MW01078436

Dark Laughter

Dark Laughter

The Satiric Art of Oliver W. Harrington

From the

Walter O. Evans

Collection of African-American Art

Edited, with an Introduction, by

M. Thomas Inge

University Press of Mississippi
Jackson

Bootsie by Ollie Harrington, *The People's Voice*, 8 August 1942

Manufactured in the United States of America

96 95 94 93 4 3 2 1

The paper in this book meets the guidelines for permanence and durability of the Committee on Production Guidelines for Book Longevity of the Council on Library Resources.

Library of Congress Cataloging-in-Publication Data

Harrington, Oliver, 1913–
Dark laughter : satiric art of Oliver W. Harrington : from the Walter O. Evans collection of African-American art / edited with an introduction by M. Thomas Inge.
p. cm.
ISBN 0-87805-656-4
1. Harrington, Oliver, 1913– —Themes, motives. 2. Afro-Americans—Caricatures and cartoons. 3. Evans, Walter O.—Art collections. 4. Caricatures and cartoons—Private collections—United States. I. Inge, M. Thomas. II. Title.
NC1429.H333A4 1993
741.5'973—dc20 93-2091
CIP

British Library Cataloging-in-Publication data available

Acknowledgments

Several people have been helpful in the completion of this volume, the most important of whom has been Dr. Walter O. Evans of Detroit. His curatorial instincts and keen interest in his heritage have led to the development of an impressive collection of African-American art and culture without which this book would not be possible. He has been a congenial collaborator. Christine McKay of the Schomburg Center for Research in Black Culture of the New York Public Library has generously shared her own research on Harrington with me and made the introduction much more accurate. We look forward to the results of her continuing investigation. The person who initially sparked the project was Lucy S. Caswell, the inimitable Director of the Cartoon, Graphic, and Photographic Arts Research Library at Ohio State University in Columbus. As always, Seetha A-Srinivasan of the University Press of Mississippi is the best editor an academic could ask for and better than most deserve. Other people who have provided essential support include Ed Black of Youngstown, Ohio; Bonnie J. Gabowitz of White Plains, New York; Shelley Armitage of Vega, Texas; Martha Gilstrap of Huntsville, Alabama; Ruth Brent of Columbia, Missouri; and Kristina Wilhite, Nancy B. Newins, Joanne H. Snapp, and Betty Lacy, all of Ashland, Virginia. Ollie Harrington is to be thanked too for allowing us to chronicle his career and pay some overdue attention to his accomplishment as a major American comic artist.

Introduction

The story of the African-American cartoonist and the American newspaper is largely an invisible history which remains to be recovered, mainly because of the lack of documentation, research, and interest on the part of cultural historians. Cartoons and comic strips are usually considered inconsequential materials, despite their close relationship to the interests and concerns of everyday people at all social and economic levels. The first black editorial cartoonist may have been Henry Jackson Lewis (1837-1891), a former slave who drew for *The Arkansas Freeman*, which billed itself as "The Only Pictorial Colored Newspaper in America." The record thereafter is almost blank until the advent of large circulation newspapers and magazines especially published for black communities.

After the turn of the century, comic strips and cartoons had become permanent parts of the mainstream newspapers; thus many editors of black newspapers encouraged the development of such features by staff artists for their readers. While often derivative and keyed to local concerns, they were more sensitive to the nuances of black life and character than anything found in the national periodicals. One of the earliest and most consistently published comic strips, which ran for over forty years from 1920 to 1963, was *Bungleton Green* in the Chicago *Defender* and reprinted elsewhere. The creator, Leslie L. Rogers, was succeeded by at least three artists, Henry Brown 1929 to 1934, Jay Jackson 1934 to 1954, and Chester Commodore for the remainder of its existence. The title character was a vaudeville-style opportunist, out to con an advantage or a fast buck, in the manner of Mutt and Jeff or Barney Google. His tenacity and spunk made him a favorite among readers often themselves on the edge of economic survival. In the 1940s *Bungleton Green* became an adventure and science fiction strip under the versatile hand of Jay Jackson, who also did a second feature called *Speed Jaxon*, more on the model of Alex Raymond's science fiction epic *Flash Gordon*.[1]

In the wake of the success of *Bungleton Green*, other features appeared in the 1930s,

An example of *Bungleton Green*, the longest-running African-American comic strip, as drawn by Chester Commodore. Chicago *Defender*, 9–15 September 1961.

such as *Sunnyboy Sam* by Wilbert Holloway, *Society Sue* and *Bucky* by Samuel Milai, and *Susabelle* by Elton Fax. *Bucky* and *Susabelle* were like a great many popular strips about children in the mainstream press, but these addressed the world of the black child with honesty and compassion. The 1940s and 1950s saw a greater versatility in such strips as Mel Tapley's teenage *Breezy*, Chester Commodore's family humor feature *The Sparks*, and a strikingly drawn feature about the achievements of the past, *Tommy Traveler in the World of Negro History* by artist Tom Feelings. There were panel cartoons exploring the humorous circumstances of black life by Ted Shearer and E. Simms Campbell. The latter would go on to greater fame with cartoons about white chorus girls and gold diggers in *Esquire*, *Playboy*, and the syndicated panel *Cuties*, most readers unaware that he was black. The most noteworthy feature of the time was *Torchy Brown* by Jackie Ormes, one of the few black female cartoonists. From 1937 to 1940, Torchy escaped discrimination and rape in the South by going to New York City, where she danced at the Cotton Club and had a variety of adventures. She returned to the newspapers from 1950 to 1955 to become more centrally involved in fighting racial and

Sunnyboy Sam by Wilbert Holloway used some of the same racially stereotyped images for blacks found in strips by white cartoonists. This particular example flirts with traditional sexual and social taboos in American society. Note the presence of numbers meant as tips for readers playing the illegal daily numbers lottery. Pittsburgh *Courier*, 15 October 1932.

Harlem Sketches : : By E. Simms Campbell

An example of *Harlem Sketches* by E. Simms Campbell before he abandoned African-American themes for cartoons about white chorus girls and young women which made him a nationally admired artist. New York *Amsterdam News*, 1 July 1935.

social problems. She served as an early and attractive model for independence among young black women. This brief outline barely touches on the highlights of those years.

By the 1960s, several cartoonists achieved mainstream distribution through national syndicates—*Wee Pals* by Morrie Turner beginning in 1964, *Luther* by Brumsic Brandon, Jr., in 1968, and *Quincy* by Ted Shearer two years later. These were all strips about children, the most consistently popular type of strip in the history of the comics. These artists' styles were radically different from each other, however, and they taught readers of all races what life looked like from the point of view of the black child growing up in a racially divided society. More importantly, they demonstrated how humor with an ethnic base could be made appealing to a national audience without recourse to the visual stereotypes of the past.

By the 1980s, syndicates were actually recruiting young black cartoonists for the greatly expanded markets for ethnically diverse features. Among the most popular to emerge have been *Curtis* by Ray Billingsley in 1988, a family strip which does not hesitate to address such social problems as drugs, drinking, and smoking (which brings the expected letters of criticism from readers who think that comics should do no more than entertain); *Jump Start* by Robb Armstrong in 1988, about the trials of a young black couple trying to get ahead in an urban community; and *Herb & Jamaal* by Stephen Bentley in 1989, which derives its humor from the experiences of two friends, former high school buddies, who view the passing scene from the advantage of an ice cream parlor they have opened. All reflect a feel for inner-city culture and streetwise language but find comedy in basic human fallibility. The most recent addition to these features is *Where I'm Coming From* in 1991 by Barbara Brandon, the daughter of Brumsic Brandon, Jr. This is an open panel cartoon about a community of friends who talk about race, sex, and politics from the perspectives of black women raised in the open society of the past two decades. There are only heads, to de-emphasize the traditional focus on the female body in the comics, and the humor is provocative but sensitively keyed to contemporary issues.

And then there is Oliver Wendell Harrington, whose career spans the entire period of history outlined here. But his story is a special and unusual one, unlike that of any of his contemporary cartoonists from the 1930s to the present.

Given the few successful practicing black cartoonists in America during Harrington's youth, he had no role models to turn to for inspiration, and much of what he saw in the comic strips of his time, he didn't like. Throughout the history of the comics, the artists were given to drawing racial stereotypes, whether the characters were Irish, Jewish, Asian, Italian, or African-American. For visual humor to be effective, as in editorial cartoons or comic strips, it tends to reduce the target of the satire or joke to a recognizable, generic image, which in turn unfortunately can become a negative stereotype. When Harrington read the funny papers in the New York *Daily News*, he has recalled, black faces "were always represented as a circle, black with two hotdogs in the middle for a mouth. . . . It was a conscious effort on my part to change that at least in my drawing. The black had to disappear. The rubber lips had to disappear."[2]

But there were deeper things that motivated Harrington to succeed in a profession which few of his race had entered than an effort to bring more faithful portrayals of blacks to the comics. These go back to his family and birthplace and the experiences he had as a child growing up in a race-conscious America during the first half of the twentieth century.

Oliver Wendell Harrington was born 14 February 1912, in the small community of Valhalla in Westchester County north of New York City. The construction of dams and reservoirs near Valhalla attracted day laborers, many of them recent European immigrants, as well as African-Americans like his father from North Carolina, among the first generation of blacks to be born as freemen. His mother, Eugenia Turat, was of Jewish descent from Budapest, Hungary. Thus Harrington grew up in a cosmopolitan household with an unusual admixture of American and European influences. He remembers an idyllic childhood, playing in the woods with the other children, exploring nearby caves, and telling ghost stories as the thunder rolled over the Hudson Valley as it must have in the days of Washington Irving. While the various ethnic groups had gathered into miniature ghettos, Harrington grew up unable to remember which of his friends were white or black.

When he was about seven, the Harrington family, consisting of his parents, two brothers (a sister would come later), and himself, moved to the South Bronx into an ethnically diverse neighborhood. By the time he reached the sixth grade, his racial identity was brought home to him in a particularly cruel way. He and a child named Prince Anderson found themselves the only two blacks in a class. Prince was from Fluvanna County, near Charlottesville, Virginia, where he had not been able to attend school, and thus he was ill-prepared and a behavior problem. As Harrington tells the story:

> One bright morning our teacher, a Miss McCoy, ordered us, the perpetually grinning Prince and me, to the front of the class. Pausing for several seconds she pointed her cheaply-jewelled finger with what I think she considered a very dramatic gesture at the trashbasket and said, "Never, never forget these two belong in that there trashbasket." The white kids giggled rather hesitantly at first and then fell out in peals of laughter. For those kids it must have been their first trip on the racist drug. It was several days before I managed to pull myself together.
>
> Gradually I felt an urge to draw little caricatures of Miss McCoy in the margins of my notebook—Miss McCoy being rammed into a local butcher shop meat grinding apparatus; Miss McCoy being run over by the speeding engines on the nearby New York Central Railroad tracks. I began to realize that each drawing lifted my spirits a little bit. And so I began to dream of becoming a cartoonist.[3]

Miss McCoy!

If Harrington learned the pains of racism from Miss McCoy, he was surprised to learn through the gentler ministrations of another teacher just how pervasive and unconsciously infectious racism could be:

> I began putting out a newspaper. Of course, it wasn't a real newspaper, but it looked like one. It was painstakingly done by hand, six columns, tabloid size with what I considered all the news of our neighborhood and with little drawings to look like photographs in a normal newspaper. I think there were six pages. My little classmates with eager eyes waited once a month to get their hands on the paper, and I enjoyed this immensely. In one column, I'd written about "Jewtown," the usual term used to describe a definite part of the Bronx community. A few days later, one of my teachers, a Mrs. Linsky, asked me to stop by for a few minutes after school so that we could talk about something.
>
> She fixed her gentle, dark eyes upon mine and this shook me up because I saw affection and interest in her eyes. And she explained the evil purpose lurking behind terms like "Jewtown" and "Niggertown." I made the association quickly. My mother was Jewish, she was Hungarian from Budapest and here I was writing about "Jewtown." This tore me to pieces. She said gently putting her fingers on her lips, "You see Oliver, people often say things without thinking—in this way they harm other people without meaning to, and one day it becomes a habit."[4]

Mrs. Linsky did even more than tutor the young Harrington in the subtle evils of racism. She provided him with his first encouragement as an artist:

> After that day we talked about many things until one day I shyly showed her some of my drawings. She stared at them for a long time and then she leaned forward in her chair placing one hand softly on my shoulder again. "Oliver," she said, "they are very, very good, and never believe anyone who says they are not." But there was a great sadness in her eyes which I did not understand. I have learned to understand it since.[5]

The sadness, of course, derived from her awareness of what a young black faced in pursuing artistic goals in a segregated society. Black children were usually persuaded to seek vocational training and careers in service and labor, but Harrington would persist in his dream.

He continued to draw throughout his years at DeWitt Clinton High School, from which he graduated in 1929 at the height of the Depression when any sort of work was hard to find. He pursued free-lance work, and by the time he was twenty, he had succeeded in placing editorial cartoons in two black newspapers, *The National News* published by George Schuyler and the *New York State Contender*. Two cartoons published in the 10 March 1932 issue of *The National News* remonstrate blacks to take their destinies in their own hands. Both are signed "O. Wendell Harrington." Another two published in October in the *Contender* call for black voters to defeat Herbert Hoover and the Republicans in favor of electing Franklin Delano Roosevelt as president.[6] While obviously the work of an apprentice, all demonstrate skill in the use of pen and ink and an effective command of the symbols and traditions of editorial cartooning. Already he had abandoned the stereotypical ways of portraying blacks, true to his earlier promise. The

Get Yourself a Job, Mr. Voter!

Never mind the sleek appointees holding jobs in Washington
Organize in your home district where the jobs for you are won
A windbag there in a swirel chair is a pretty sight to witness
But a solid hold on the home payroll will better aid your business.

One of Harrington's earliest published drawings, an editorial cartoon for the *National News*, 10 March 1932. Courtesy the Schomburg Center for Research in Black Culture of the New York Public Library, Scrapbook Collection.

Handkerchief-Head Negroes Must Go

An early editorial cartoon signed "O. Wendell Harrington," his first signature. *National News*, 10 March 1932. Courtesy the Schomburg Center for Research in Black Culture of the New York Public Library, Scrapbook Collection.

"—Home to Roost"

An early editorial cartoon signed "Ol Harrington," his signature for most of his career. *The New York State Contender*, 22 October 1932. Courtesy the Schomburg Center for Research in Black Culture of the New York Public Library, Scrapbook Collection.

An early editorial cartoon for *The New York State Contender*. The date has been torn from the clipping, but it is probably around October 1932. Courtesy the Schomburg Center for Research in Black Culture of the New York Public Library, Scrapbook Collection.

October cartoons were signed "Ol Harrington," a signature he would use for most of his career until it became "Ollie Harrington."

By the time these early efforts appeared, Harrington had left home to live in Harlem, where he found a room at the YMCA for two dollars a week. For a creative young black man, Harlem was the most exciting place imaginable. Beginning in the 1920s, this section of upper Manhattan founded by Peter Stuyvesant had become the center of the most dazzling group of black writers, painters, musicians, scholars, and intellectuals ever assembled in America. Encouraged by activist W.E.B. DuBois and philosopher Alain Locke, such writers as Claude McKay, Langston Hughes, Jean Toomer, Rudolph Fisher, Countee Cullen, James Weldon Johnson, Arna Bontemps, and Zora Neale Hurston were producing a remarkable body of poetry, fiction, and prose which addressed the nature of black identity in America, established a place for black writers in mainstream publishing, and defined the period known as the Harlem Renaissance which would influence all of American art and culture to come.

Although the period of high productivity was over when Harrington arrived on the scene, he flourished in the afterglow of their example. While an intellectual like Locke remained somewhat aloof from the young cartoonist, he became close friends with several of the writers, including Bontemps, Fisher, Wallace Thurman, and especially Langston Hughes. Probably the most accomplished and widely published of the Harlem

Boop, Harrington's first effort at a comic strip. Pittsburgh *Courier*, 11 March 1933.

figures and versatile in his talents, Hughes took Harrington under his wing, encouraged his artistic interests, and would remain a steadfast supporter and friend throughout his life. When Harrington published a book of his cartoons in 1958, Hughes wrote the introduction for it, and he would pay Harrington high compliments in public and print.

Harrington received a small scholarship and began taking classes at the National Academy of Design in drawing and painting while he worked at a variety of jobs to support himself: creating a puppet show, playing minor parts in an opera version of *The Emperor Jones*, designing stage props, and working in an employment agency among them. Following the 1932 political cartoons he had published, he began to receive assignments from the New York *Amsterdam News*, the major black newspaper in the New York area, as well as such influential papers as the Baltimore *Afro-American* and the Pittsburgh *Courier*. The *Courier* would prove to be a major venue for his work for the next thirty years.

His earliest contribution to the *Courier* was a comic strip called *Boop* on 11 March 1933, about a typical classroom prank, but the following week, on 18 March it became a regular series called *Scoop* featuring the mishaps of a small child much in the style of Percy Crosby's *Skippy*, then America's favorite comic strip about a forlorn waif and subject of a popular film which launched the career of child-star Jackie Coogan in 1931. At first a simple gag strip, on 29 March Harrington turned it into a melodramatic continuing narrative about Scoop's wicked stepmother who suspects that his dead

Harrington's first sustained comic strip, *Scoop*, was about children, the favorite topic for humor in the American comic strip. His style here appears to have been modeled after Percy Crosby in *Skippy*, which was then very popular. Pittsburgh *Courier*, 1 April 1933.

father left him a lot of money which he has hidden. After she beats him and chains him to his bed, he escapes and hits the road with his stepmother and a criminal accomplice in pursuit. The story has much in common with the widely read orphan adventure strips of the period, such as *Little Orphan Annie* by Harold Gray or *Little Annie Rooney* drawn by Darrell McClure, with a touch of Charles Dickens and Mark Twain's Huckleberry Finn thrown in. Harrington was learning his way to his own style and subject matter by drawing on the prevailing sentiments of the day. *Scoop* was more original, in any case, than those around him in the *Courier* on the comics page—Wilbert Holloway's *Sunnyboy Sam*, Bob Pious's *The Dupes*, Bill Chase's *Betty*, or Raymond Henry's *Bonnie*—all of which were imitative of the mainstream American comic strips of the gag and family humor variety.

It was in the pages of the *Amsterdam News* that Bootsie, his best-loved creation, first saw the light of day. On 18 May 1935, the editors announced an expanded and improved

After following the gag-a-day format, Harrington turned *Scoop* into a melodramatic narrative on the model of Harold Gray's *Little Orphan Annie*, with a touch of Charles Dickens and Mark Twain. Pittsburgh *Courier*, 29 April 1933.

Dark Laughter : : : By OL' HARRINGTON

"Comrades, fellow workers!"

A *Dark Laughter* panel before the advent of Bootsie. Many had a strong political orientation, like this one. New York *Amsterdam News*, 28 September 1935.

edition of the weekly at ten cents "With These Outstanding Artists and Writers." Among the sixteen contributors listed and pictured in the full-page advertisement were four cartoonists: E. Simms Campbell, prominently featured and the best known at the time; William Charles Chase, the art director; the prolific Jay Jackson; and Ol Harrington. Beginning in the newly inaugurated tabloid section, *New York Amsterdam News Magazine*, on 25 May, Harrington's first *Dark Laughter* panel appeared, alongside a full-page series of cartoons by Campbell called *Harlem Sketches*, a small panel by Chase about modern young women appropriately titled *Modernettes*, and what would prove to be a long-running illustrated serial novel by Jackson about an exotic woman named *Tisha Mingo* (which opens interestingly in a Chicago bawdy house).

From the start, *Dark Laughter* had the realistic feel of experienced urban life, based as it was on the "almost unbelievable but hilarious chaos" Harrington said he saw around him in Harlem.[7] There was no recognizable cast of characters in the beginning, and given the enormous supply of absurd incidents and picturesque people he met daily, he felt that the cartoons almost drew themselves. Then, naturally and inevitably it seemed that something happened, as Harrington has told it:

> After a while a jolly, rather well fed but soulful character emerged and crept into each drawing. Ted Poston, the world's loudest and fastest-talking journalist, who was city editor of the *Amsterdam*, named the character Bootsie and Bootsie it has been ever since. And I was more surprised than anyone when Brother Bootsie became a Harlem household celebrity, not only among the colored proletariat but among the literati as well.[8]

While he was bringing Bootsie into being, he was simultaneously preparing a feature called *Pages from Negro History* by Africanus, modeled after Robert L. Ripley's *Believe It or Not* with little-known vignettes about black history, and drawing sports cartoons. Later, in August 1936, when staff artist Bill Chase was sent to Berlin to cover the Olympics, Harrington substituted for him with editorial cartoons, portraits, and other illustrative tasks usually handled by Chase.

The first appearance and use of the name "Bootsie" was in a *Dark Laughter* panel for 28 December 1935, in which two disreputable looking men, one heavy and one thin, are speaking to three clerks in a liquor store who have brought out bottles of their most expensive wares. The thin fellow says, "Naw Mister. Me an' Bootsie jus' wants some plain corn." Bootsie and his unnamed buddy would appear in nearly every cartoon afterwards in the *Amsterdam News*, and Bootsie's character would gradually take on definite lineaments. The anchor of a specific character worked to provide Harrington with a convenient beginning point for his humor.

Bootsie is a stout, bald, and mustachioed man who finds himself at the center of some comic situation which he has either initiated or unwittingly walked into. A lover of fine soul food, liquor, and women, either by comment or silent witness, he reflects on the fads and foibles of the urban black community, and as often as not, he himself is the butt of the humor. Racism and conflict with the white community frequently serve as

Dark Laughter . . . *By OL HARRINGTON*

"The party was leapin' until Bootsie here got playful."

The second appearance of Bootsie in a *Dark Laughter* panel. New York *Amsterdam News*, 4 January 1936.

the main topic, but much of the ridicule is directed at blacks themselves and the way they treat each other. It is this internal satire that moves the target of the humor in the direction of human nature and gives Harrington's comic skills the broadest social relevance and universal applicability. Bootsie and his friends, many of whom become regular characters and take center stage in Bootsie's absence, are like everyone attempting to reconcile the contradictions and absurdities of their daily lives, especially the incongruity between the American dream and the nation's failure to fulfill it. Harrington has admitted that there was a lot of himself in Bootsie and a critique therefore of his own human weaknesses.

While there may be much of Falstaff and Sancho Panza in his constitution, Bootsie is also a part of the American tradition of the wise fool, the clown whose antics and comments contain more than a little wisdom and common sense. Harrington's friend, Langston Hughes, would develop the character most fully in African-American literature in his Jesse B. Semple sketches in his weekly newspaper columns beginning in 1943 and later collected into five books. Both Bootsie and "Simple" are urban everymen whose actions and comments puncture the pomposities of those trying to get ahead in a racist society through ruse and compromise. Hughes once expressed admiration for Harrington's ability to convey in one drawing what it took him thousands of words to say.

Everyone who knew anything about black life and culture during the mid-century in America knew about Bootsie, the first black newspaper comic character to achieve a national reputation. When Harrington met Paul Robeson, the singer boomed, "Feller, I just wanted you to know that those cartoons of yours are great."[9] In his 1958 introduction to *Bootsie and Others*, Langston Hughes declared:

> Harrington has long been Negro America's favorite cartoonist. . . . As a social satirist in the field of race relations, Ollie Harrington is unsurpassed. Visually funny almost always, situation-wise, his pictures frequently have the quality of the blues. Behind the humor often lurks the sadness of "When you see me laughin', I'm laughin' to keep from cryin'." . . . A careful craftsman, an excellent satirist, with a little of Daumier and a lot of Hogarth—although not really very much like either, being too full of laughter—Ollie Harrington is uniquely Harrington, and Bootsie of Harlem is out of this world.[10]

The name Bootsie was so well known in New York at one time that when Orson Welles suggested that a young black actor call himself Bootsie Washington, it spelled his success as a comic dramatist in Welles's theater. Harrington would draw the character for almost thirty years for several publications—the Pittsburgh *Courier*, *The People's Voice*, the Chicago *Defender*, and the Baltimore *Afro-American* among them—and Bootsie was a major contribution to American humor and comic art.

In 1936, Harrington had enrolled in Yale University's School of the Fine Arts, thinking that he might become a painter or a teacher of art history while he continued to perfect his cartooning. Yale had been one of the first American universities to establish a separate school of fine arts, and by the time Harrington was enrolled, *Life* magazine could report, "Today's Yale offers the most complete art education in this country. In its rigorous five-year courses, students learn everything from drawing apples to designing railroad stations. Tradition and technique are the watchwords at Yale."[11] Harrington would always be grateful for the training and discipline he acquired at Yale, which he felt strengthened his professional work. Yale in turn would be proud of him. Shortly after he graduated in 1940 with a BFA degree and had begun work on an MFA, *Life* reporters came to Yale to do the above quoted article. In one photograph of a group of students, Harrington is only one of two mentioned by name in the caption, and his color painting "Deep South" was one of four student works selected for reproduction in *Life*.[12]

According to the caption for "Deep South," Harrington admitted to the influence of El Greco and Thomas Hart Benton, which clearly shows, but the painting also displays a considerable command of the tools of brush, oils, and canvas and reflects the kind of dignity he wished to portray in his depictions of black characters. With the pay he was receiving for his Bootsie cartoons, newspaper work, scholarships, and occasional jobs like washing dishes at a New Haven fraternity house, Harrington made ends meet. He was awarded a Yale University European Fellowship, but the German invasion of Poland and the beginning of World War II canceled the opportunity and further work on his MFA degree.

Harrington always seemed to cross paths with the most prominent black leaders in both the creative and political arenas. In February, 1942, Adam Clayton Powell, Jr., fresh from his successes as a civil rights activist and the vocal pastor of the Abyssinian Baptist Church, founded with Harlem businessman Charles Buchanan a new weekly newspaper, *The People's Voice*. Although rumored to have been funded by financier Marshall Field, the newspaper promptly took a radical stance and called itself "a working class paper" that was "100% owned and operated by Negroes." At a time when the Soviet Union and America were wartime allies, Powell even described *The People's Voice* as the "Lenox Avenue edition of the *Daily Worker*."[13]

Powell gave Harrington his first full-time job as the art director, and beginning with the first issue published on Frederick Douglass's birthday, 14 February 1942, every weekly edition of *The People's Voice* would contain Harrington's editorial cartoons, illustrations, humorous cartoons, and even a comic strip. Of course, he brought Bootsie with him under the title *Dark Laughter*, and the editors noted, "Beginning with this [first] issue of the Voice the nationally famed character Bootsie will appear on this page," just below Powell's famed "Soap Box" column which he transferred from the *Amsterdam News*. The note continued, "The Voice is the only paper in the New York area which, in the future, will carry the cartoon." Harrington also began a comic strip called *Jive Gray* about a "star reporter on the 'Liberator,' one of America's couragious [*sic*] race papers." Just as Jive is sent out to investigate a series of dangerous threats to his paper, the

Harrington was the art director and editorial cartoonist for *The People's Voice*. This example is from the second issue, 28 February 1942. The paradox of young black men fighting against European fascism and racism abroad while experiencing discrimination at home was a frequent theme of African-American commentary at the time.

feature was stopped after only three weeks, but Harrington would remember the hero's name and use it again for another comic strip the following year.

In a prophetic conjunction, the first issue of *The People's Voice* began a serialization of Richard Wright's *Native Son* with illustrations by Harrington, almost a decade before he would meet Wright and become his closest friend. Published two years earlier, the novel had attracted considerable critical attention in both mainstream and black publications. Most white reviewers recognized the artistic power and social truth of Wright's first novel, even though they were disturbed by the social tensions it uncovered. In the black press the critics were proud of Wright's accomplishment as their first recognized major novelist, but they were concerned that the violent protagonist Bigger Thomas would be seen as a fulfillment of the larger society's worst fears and prejudices. This controversy would follow upon Powell's decision to reprint the novel, which he had warmly praised in an earlier "Soap Box" column for the *Amsterdam News* on 16 March 1940.

When the seventh installment appeared in the issue for 28 March 1942, the letters column carried a communication from a Harold P. Joyner, who complained, "I think you have made a big mistake by reprinting 'Native Son.' Plenty of Negro and white families would not buy a book containing every swear word you could call, and put it in their houses where there are children. 'Tobacco Road' has had no reprint in any white newspaper." No installment appeared in the 4 April issue, and instead there was a notice "Announcing Postcard Poll," inviting readers to vote by postcard whether the serialization should continue because so many complaints were being received about the lan-

FEBRUARY 14, 1942 — THE PEOPLE'S VOICE — 35

NATIVE SON

Richard WRIGHT

INSTALLMENT I

Brrrrrriiiiiiiiiiiiiiiiiinng!

An alarm clock clanged in the dark and silent room. A bed spring creaked. A woman's voice sang out impatiently:

"Bigger, shut that thing off!"

A surly grunt sounded above the tinny ring of metal. Naked feet swished dryly across the planks in the wooden floor and the clang ceased abruptly.

"Turn on the light, Bigger."

"Awright," came a sleepy mumble.

Light flooded the room and revealed a black boy standing in a narrow space between two iron beds, rubbing his eyes with the backs of his hands. From a bed to his right the woman spoke again:

"Buddy, get up from there! I got a big washing on my hands today and I want you-all out of here."

Another black boy rolled from bed and stood up. The woman also rose and stood in her nightgown.

"Turn your heads so I can dress," she said.

The two boys averted their eyes and gazed into a far corner of the room. The woman rushed out of her nightgown and put on a pair of step-ins. She turned to the bed from which she had risen and called:

"Vera! Get up from there!"

"What time is it, Ma?" asked a muffled, adolescent voice from beneath a quilt.

"Get up from there, I say!"

[illegible] girl in a cotton [illegible] got up and stretched her [illegible] above her head and yawned. Sleepily, she sat on a chair and fumbled with her stockings. The two boys kept their faces averted while their mother and sister put on enough clothes to keep them from feeling ashamed; and the mother and sister did the same while the boys dressed. Abruptly, they all paused, holding their clothes in their hands, their attention caught by a light tapping in the thinly plastered walls of the room. They forgot their conspiracy against shame and their eyes strayed apprehensively over the floor.

"There he is again, Bigger!" the woman screamed, and the tiny, one-room apartment galvanized into violent action. A chair toppled as the woman, half-dressed and in her stocking feet, scrambled breathlessly upon the bed. Her two sons, barefoot, stood tense and motionless, their eyes searching anxiously under the bed and chairs. The girl ran into a corner, half-stooped and gathered the hem of her slip into both of her hands and held it tightly over her knees.

"Oh! Oh!" she wailed.

"There he goes!"

The woman pointed a shaking finger. Her eyes were round with fascinated horror.

"Where?"

"I don't see 'im!"

"Bigger, he's behind the trunk!" the girl whimpered.

"Vera!" the woman screamed.

Get up here on the bed! Don't let that thing *bite* you!"

Frantically, Vera climbed up on the bed and the woman caught hold of her. With their arms entwined about each other, the black mother and the brown daughter gazed open-mouthed at the trunk in the corner.

Bigger looked round the room wildly, then darted to a curtain and swept it aside and grabbed two heavy iron skillets from a wall above a gas stove. He whirled and called softly to his brother, his eyes glued to the trunk.

"Buddy!"

"Yeah?"

"Here; take this skillet."

"O.K."

"Now, get over by the door!"

"O.K."

Buddy crouched by the door and held the iron skillet by its handle, his arm flexed and poised. Save for the quick, deep breathing of the four people, the room was quiet. Bigger crept on tiptoe toward the trunk with the skillet clutched stiffly in his hand, his eyes dancing and watching every inch of the wooden floor in front of him. He paused and, without moving an eye or muscle, called:

"Buddy!"

"Hunh?"

"Put that box in front of the hole so he can't get out!"

"O.K."

Buddy ran to a wooden box and shoved it quickly in front of a gaping hole in the molding and then backed again to the door, holding the skillet ready. Bigger eased to the trunk and peered behind it cautiously. He saw nothing. Carefully, he stuck out his bare foot and pushed the trunk a few inches.

"There he is!" the mother screamed again.

A huge black rat squealed and leaped at Bigger's trouser-leg and snagged it in his teeth, hanging on.

"Goddamn!" Bigger whispered fiercely, whirling and kicking out his leg with all the strength of his body. The force of his movement shook the rat loose and it sailed through the air and struck a wall. Instantly, it rolled over and leaped again. Bigger dodged and the rat landed against a table leg. With clenched teeth, Bigger held the skillet; he was afraid to hurl it, fearing that he might miss. The rat squeaked and turned and ran in a narrow circle, looking for a place to hide; it leaped again past Bigger and scurried on dry rasping feet to one side of the box and then to the other, searching for the hole. Then it turned and reared upon its h legs.

"Hit 'im, Bigger!" Buddy sho

"Kill 'im!" the woman scre

The rat's belly pulsed with

Bigger advanced a step and th emitted a long thin song of ance, its black beady eyes gl ing, its tiny forefeet pawing the restlessly. Bigger swung the sk let; it skidded over the floor, mi ing the rat, and clattered to a st against the wall.

"Goddamn!"

The rat leaped. Bigger sprang to one side. The rat stopped under a chair and let out a furious screak. Bigger moved slowly backward toward the door.

"Gimme that skillet, Buddy," he asked quietly, not taking his eyes from the rat.

Buddy extended his hand. Bigger caught the skillet and lifted it high in the air. The rat scuttled across the floor and stopped again at the box and searched quickly for the hole; then it reared once more and bared long yellow fangs, piping shrilly, belly quivering.

Bigger aimed and let the skillet fly with a heavy grunt. There was a shattering of wood as the box caved in. The woman screamed and hid her face in her hands. Bigger tiptoed forward and peered.

(Continued Next Week)

"HIT 'IM, BIGGER!" BUDDY SHOUTED.

JIVE GRAY — OL HARRINGTON

This page from the first issue of Adam Clayton Powell, Jr.'s newspaper featured the first installment of Richard Wright's novel *Native Son*, with illustration by Harrington, and the first installment of the short-lived early version of the comic strip *Jive Gray*. *The People's Voice*, 14 February 1942.

guage. Finally on 18 April, beneath a sketch of a coffin labeled "Native Son" being placed in an open grave, the following notice appeared:

REQUIESCAT IN PACE

The editors of PV, like "Miss Otis," regret that Richard Wright's best selling novel, "Native Son," is, as of this issue, laid to rest at the behest of post-carding readers of this par-excellent paper. Several complaints had come in to PV, objecting to the profanity used in the story. PV goes into homes of all sorts—religious folk, worldly cats. So-o-o-o-o, we asked readers to send in postcards on their reactions to our continuing to publish "Son." The choice was thus left to those who were reading the story (PV editors read the book when first published).

Result of the poll: "Son" was too damn profane. Hence, briefly, "Son" is herewith deceased, demised, done to death. PV's editors' opinion: Wright did a swell piece of writing on"Son," will do more and better writing. PV thot "Son" a piece of writing worth reading, advises its fans to BUY a copy and read it, believing it worth while. In killing "Son," PV insists 'twas only because of the profanity, etc.

The paper published only one brief response to this action in a letter to the editor on 16 May 1942, from Addie Beverly of Staten Island: "I feel that in spite of the language used throughout 'Native Son,' everyone should read the book."

Adam Clayton Powell, Jr., seemingly misremembered this incident when he told Keneth Kinnamon in a 1968 interview that "when Max Yergan bought Powell's newspaper, *People's Voice*, he dropped the serialization of *Native Son* that Powell had begun because of [Communist] party discontent with Wright."[14] The fact is that Powell did not resign his position as editor and sell his stock in *The People's Voice* until 10 December 1946, over four years after the novel was banished from its pages.[15] If the Communist party somehow had a hand in the newspaper poll, there is no evidence of it.

Harrington's drawings reflected a genuine affinity for the harsh detail and grim reality of Wright's novel, but the collaboration was not to be, as a prudish readership evidently banned a masterpiece from the pages of what was meant to be a "radical" black newspaper. In another context, this was the sort of self-defeating internal contradiction in the black community which would often form the basis for humor in a Bootsie cartoon.

Native Son was not the only source of reader complaint, since Harrington's work elicited criticism. In the 21 March 1942 issue, he had drawn a cartoon series satirizing the flashy and extreme zoot suits popular in the black community, and the 28 March issue contained a letter from Marian Williams stating, "Harrington certainly got off base with that jitterbug series of drawings last week, showing those extreme suits, etc. Of all the important things for your paper to consider, why waste space on anything like that." Even the widely admired Bootsie irritated another reader, a Miss Dorothy K. Williams of Brooklyn, whose letter appeared on 2 May 1942:

LAMBASTS "BOOTSIE"

Sir: Since the first issue of your excellent paper was released, I have never missed an issue. THE PEOPLE'S VOICE answered the long-felt need of the masses of the Negro

This cartoon by Harrington satirizing the contemporary trend in dress in the black community among men was criticized by one reader of Powell's newspaper. *The People's Voice*, 21 March 1942.

> people for just such a militant, aggressive weekly, which dared to go to bat for the thousands of decent, intelligent, honest American citizens of the Negro race.
>
> However, there is one thing in your paper that disturbs me no end and which I think definitely detracts from the high standard which your paper has set. I refer to the cartoons by Ol Harrington. He may be a fine artist in his field, but why must he confine his cartoons to pimps, cowards, and other such characters of the "Pee Wee" variety—the effect of which is to do nothing but belittle the Negro? It seems to me we get enough of that from the white cartoonists.

Harrington was allowed to speak in his own defense:

> With characteristic perverseness peculiar to maniacs, Southern Congressmen and cartoonists, I do not consider my cartoons low, degrading, or otherwise odiferous to the sensitive masses. I still obstinately believe that there are some imbeciles left among us who find time in between bone-pulverizing bombings, mass murder and other sadistic

14 THE PEOPLE'S VOICE OCTOBER 3, 1942

BLUES IN THE NEWS:

NEWS ITEM: Mrs. Susie Bluckotty writes, "Dear Mr. Harrington. . . . My son Bubberdoo wants to be a cartoonist. His teacher says that's about all he's good for. We would like some information about it." Well, dear madame, here it is:

Blues in the News was a regular feature by Harrington commenting on some news item of the day. In this installment, he commented on the difficulties of being a cartoonist with deadlines to meet. *The People's Voice*, 3 October 1942.

> forms of civilized recreation, to laugh. Pee Wee, Bootsie and company are harmless fun-loving beings, eternally catching hell but still coming up with a smile.

Actually, the last Bootsie cartoon had appeared in *The People's Voice* three weeks earlier, on 11 April. Whether Miss Williams' letter had anything to do with this is unknown, but it does seem that Powell's paper was highly sensitive to conservative pressure from its readers while presenting a radical, militant face to the larger public and opponents of racial progress. That the paper held Harrington in high regard, however, is confirmed by an admiring feature article on the cartoonist in the issue for 8 August 1942, where he is ranked with "the best of contemporary humorists and cartoonists" practicing in America.

Harrington continued to contribute to *The People's Voice* through the issue for 17 July 1943, including a three-part word and picture story on the black Third Army's war games in Louisiana on 15, 22, and 29 May, his first field assignment with the military. After his departure from the paper, other artists were called on to fill in for Harrington's regular features, including a young Ted Shearer, but it was not until October that they found someone who could reasonably reproduce Harrington's style, a cartoonist named John Robertson. This attempt to find an imitator was in itself a kind of tribute and acknowledgment that he was irreplaceable, and some less attentive readers probably didn't even know he was gone. Presumably he had been lured away by the Pittsburgh *Courier* with the promise of more exciting assignments.

In any case, the *Courier* put him to work immediately on several projects, one of

Illustration for an article about "Southernism" in *The People's Voice*, 24 October 1942.

An illustration for Harrington's news story "Army Air Force," about the black 332nd Fighter Group at Selfridge Field, Michigan. Pittsburgh *Courier*, 30 October 1943.

which he had begun while still in the employ of *The People's Voice*. At the time, the weekly black-and-white comics page mainly consisted of panel cartoons by Ted Shearer and E. Simms Campbell and the standby comic strips *Sunnyboy Sam* by Wilbert Holloway and *Society Sue* and *Bucky* by Samuel Milai, so Harrington was asked to develop a new adventure feature with a war setting. Like most cartoonists of that period faced with the challenge of drawing an adventure strip, he turned to the master of intrigue and realism in the comics, Milton Caniff. Since 1934, Caniff's *Terry and the Pirates* had beguiled thousands of readers with stories about such characters as soldier of fortune Pat Ryan, his young companion Terry, their Chinese partner Connie, and the numerous voluptuous women Caniff drew so well, including the deadly Dragon Lady. Caniff's penchant for authentic backgrounds, authoritative detail, and realistic rendition set a new standard in comic strip art, and few could escape its influence.

When Harrington's *Jive Gray* appeared in the *Courier* on 8 May 1943, the influence of Caniff was apparent in the style of drawing and the dramatically staged figures as a group of fighter pilots are sent aloft to encounter a fleet of Nazi bombers with the injunction, "Remember they say that they don't know whether Negroes make good pilots. You can make them liars!" While many strips to follow reflect a study of Caniff's use of camera angles, point of view, and visual design, Harrington obviously has done

An early statement by Harrington on the topic of apartheid in South Africa before the word gained currency around 1945. *The People's Voice*, 14 November 1942.

his homework and incorporates places and people out of his own research and experience. He also demonstrates that he knows how to plot and tell a story with the kind of narrative pace and suspense demanded by the conventions of comic strip literature.

Harrington even anticipates his instructor in a story beginning 24 February 1945. Jive Gray is sent on a secret mission into collapsing Germany where he abandons his plane to parachute to an encounter with a group of Russian soldiers led by Col. Pushkin, a formidable female commander in the mold of the Dragon Lady. As the war approaches a conclusion, she proposes that Jive join her as an officer in the World Security Police which will fight fascism and promote peace into the post-war years. In one sequence,

The first installment of the *Jive Gray* comic strip. Pittsburgh *Courier*, 8 May 1943.

How Harrington would learn from and adapt the style of Milton Caniff is illustrated by these two strips, the first a *Terry and the Pirates* strip from 9 September 1942, and a *Jive Gray* from the Pittsburgh *Courier*, 18 May 1946.

Milton Caniff was a master of detail in portraying fighter planes and air warfare, and Harrington knew how to adapt his techniques for his own purposes. *Terry and the Pirates*, 19 March 1943, and Pittsburgh *Courier*, 25 September 1943.

they encounter a white racist from Mississippi who has joined the Nazi army because of their ideology. Almost two years after this sequence, on 13 January 1947, Milton Caniff would abandon *Terry and the Pirates* to begin a strip called *Steve Canyon* about a former Air Force pilot. Wanting to use his military experience in the post-war years, Canyon establishes Horizons Unlimited, dedicated to trouble-shooting throughout the world. His first employer is the beautiful and assertive Copper Calhoun. Caniff apparently was not aware of Jive Gray and his parallel situation in the earlier story, and Jive does return to full-time military service rather than remain with Pushkin's operation, but there are also striking physical similarities between the angular, pipe-smoking Jive Gray and his post-war counterpart Steve Canyon. If his readers enjoyed *Jive Gray*, they also continued to want their Bootsie cartoons, so beginning 17 February 1945, *Dark Laughter* returned to the *Courier* with a front-page announcement of the event.

The *Courier* also kept Harrington on the road. In the fall of 1943, he was sent on a tour of selected military bases in America to investigate contributions by blacks to the war effort. The first result was a full-page feature on 30 October entitled "Army Air Force," with his sketches of black fighter pilots at Selfridge Field in Michigan, especially the 332nd Fighter Group at a nearby sub-base. His highly technical renderings of P-40 Warhawk planes and the soldiers at work and play display a skill for realistic illustration which would also inform *Jive Gray*. Similar features followed.

Since the draft board had not called Harrington to military service, the *Courier* sent him abroad as a war correspondent first to North Africa and then to Europe. He preferred this since it allowed him to contribute to the allied cause without having to accept the strictures of a segregated army. On the way to North Africa, his ship was threatened by a torpedo. In Italy, he escorted Walter White, novelist and NAACP executive, to the battlefront, where they argued about whether shells were outgoing or incoming. His experiences abroad also introduced Harrington to a larger world society where race seemed less consequential in human relations.

After the war was over, Walter White asked Harrington to create a public relations department for the NAACP. He hesitated, uncertain that this was his kind of work, until a series of lynchings in the South and stories about mistreated black veterans persuaded him to take the job. He became involved especially in the case of Isaac Woodard who was dragged from a bus in South Carolina, beaten, and blinded. This led Harrington into the public political arena where he discovered an unsuspected talent for debate and speech-making.

For example, at the opening session of the New York *Herald Tribune*'s forum on "The Struggle for Justice as a World Force" on 28 October 1946, Harrington challenged then U.S. Attorney General Tom Clark who had announced a massive federal investigation of the lynching of four men at Monroe, Georgia, but still had no convictions, by declaring, "For the crime of race hate and lynching there has never been a conviction in the history of the United States." On the larger theme of the conference, Harrington forcefully stated:

> We are talking of justice and agencies of justice. In Columbia, Tennessee, where an entire Negro community was subjected to wholesale and vicious vandalism, the Department of Justice was unable to identify a single guilty person. Now, Columbia is a small town where every one knows every one else and yet the same agency that tracked every foreign spy during the last war, the greatest secret service agency in the world, was unable to find a single clue, locate a single criminal who took part in the crushing of an American community.[16]

Harrington would remain convinced that this debate was what led Clark later to label him a Communist. A month later, on 24 November, Harrington would speak at the closing session of an NAACP youth conference in New Orleans on a topic close to his heart—the rights of blacks to participate in the cultural life of the nation. According to the New York *Times*, Harrington stated:

> The Bilboes and Talmadges who exclude Negroes from a full participation in the political life of the nation are also guilty of preventing them from taking part in any of the creative forms by barring Negroes from art museums, theaters and libraries in the South.
>
> This is ironic, since the music of the South is a Negro gift to the arts, it is criminal that the creators of the arts are denied the right to participate in the enjoyment and expansion of them.
>
> The great fight upward to make first-class citizens out of the masses of our people rests upon the determination to allow them to express themselves by the standards of the finest arts.[17]

Harrington now found himself something of a public figure and no longer simply a much admired cartoonist and journalist, with unfortunate consequences. The House Un-American Activities Committee had been working since 1938 to investigate those they considered subversives in the nation, and following the temporary truce with the Soviet Union during World War II, the "witch-hunt" was renewed again with vigor, especially after 1949 with the fanatical encouragement of Senator Joseph McCarthy from Wisconsin, who claimed to have a lengthy list of "known Communists" employed by the State Department. Given its advocacy of integration and radical improvements in civil rights, the NAACP was a prime target of investigation by the FBI and other agencies. Harrington had been identified as a major spokesman for the group, so what happened was inevitable. As Harrington tells it:

> I met an old friend at the Hotel Teresa Bar which was one of the most famous and pleasant watering places for the brothers. . . .So we went in and had some drinks and after a while . . . my friend was making funny motions below the bar. I turned back to him and took a closer look. He was showing me his badge—Army Intelligence. So I wondered aloud, "Man, my old friend. What's happening?" He said, "I'm warning you to go to Europe. Take a vacation for six months and let this thing blow over." Well, he was much more optimistic than I was when he told me that. So I asked him, "How can you do

this? It's a terribly dangerous thing you're doing by telling me this." He said, "Yes, but look," and he held his hand out next to mine. Both hands were black.[18]

Despite his heavy investment of time in the NAACP, Harrington maintained his production of cartoons and drawings for the black press, taught art classes at the Jefferson School of Social Science in New York, and became art editor for the paper *Freedom* in 1950. He had already illustrated several books, including a children's book in 1942, *Hezekiah Horton* by Ellen F. Tarry. His drawings for the same author's *The Runaway Elephant* in 1950, however, brought special distinction. The cover and illustrations were selected by the American Institute of Graphic Arts in 1951 for an award in its annual competition for the Fifty Best American Books, the first time the institute had cited work by a black artist.

Late in 1951, Harrington finally took the warning of his friend to heart and left the states for France, planning to continue his painting and study art in Paris, something which had been interrupted while at Yale. Paris had already become the center for a gathering of talented black artists, writers, and intellectuals who were frustrated with life in the United States, a movement stimulated by Richard Wright who came to Paris in 1946 and which would eventually include people like novelist Chester Himes, a promising young writer named James Baldwin, painter Beauford Delaney, sculptor Howard Cousins, and William Gardner Smith, who had written a novel about African-American soldiers in Germany during the war. Many others were less well known or aspiring talents who would never achieve significant attention, but here they were free to pursue their personal lives and creativity without political or social hindrance. It was in the Cafe Tournon, where many of these people gathered for afternoon coffee, that Harrington met Richard Wright. They like each other immediately, and Harrington would remain Wright's closest friend for the rest of his life.

Given his greater fame and notoriety, one would expect Wright to be the center of attention in this gathering of black expatriates, but Chester Himes, who would also count Harrington his closest friend, has testified differently:

Ollie was the center of the American community on the Left Bank in Paris, white and black, and he was the greatest Lothario in the history of the whole Latin Quarter. And he was a fabulous raconteur too. He used to keep people spellbound for hours. So they collected there because of Ollie. Then the rest of us came.[19]

Harrington greatly enjoyed the social life and the open exchange of ideas in Paris, where people of all nationalities and races were free to pursue philosophy or friendship without prejudice. He spent time at the Grande Chaumière, a building where artists gathered to practice and to sketch from live models, and he learned to speak French. The only thing he couldn't do was get work, since the periodicals there preferred to hire their own nationals, so Harrington continued to contribute cartoons by mail to the Pittsburgh *Courier* and the Chicago *Defender*. This gave him a modest income, although, to his disappointment, the checks often bounced at the bank. That he was not forgotten in the U. S. is suggested by the appearance in 1958 from Dodd, Mead & Company of an anthology, *Bootsie and Others*, with an introduction by Langston Hughes.

Things were not always idyllic, however. Because of lingering suspicions about his politics, the American Embassy once unsuccessfully attempted to confiscate his passport and would hassle him, Wright, and others bureaucratically. He found himself involved in a dispute with another American writer named Richard Gibson, who also worked for the Pittsburgh *Courier*, which became almost legendary in the American community in Paris. As Richard Wright's biographer, Addison Gayle, related the affair:

> In 1956, Harrington had rented his apartment to a fellow black American, Richard Gibson. When Harrington returned to repossess his apartment, Gibson refused to give it up. Moreover, he laid claim to all of Harrington's personal property. Several fights erupted between the two, in which Harrington thrashed Gibson very soundly. Himes wrote of the second fight: "I was thinking about going over to Ollie's to retrieve my kitchen utensils when he and Gibson had their second fight. . . . Ollie beat up Gibson so bad that time that the police arrested him." . . . Harrington, however, was reluctant to press charges, due to his expatriate status and his reputation as a Communist sympathizer. The black community began choosing sides in the conflict. Himes and Wright supported Harrington. Gibson had the support of William Gardner Smith. In 1957, a letter attacking French policy was printed in *Life* magazine under Harrington's signature. The letter was later proved to have been a forgery, written by Gibson. Another altercation between Gibson and Harrington occurred soon after, and this time Gibson was beaten so badly that he was taken to the hospital. He later signed a confession, "but the American Embassy possibly intervened with the Sûreté Nationale to hush up the affair." Wright was involved as a friend of Harrington's and because he was called, in the spring of 1958, to testify on Harrington's behalf. His interest in the affair did not stop there. He kept documents of the investigation, wrote a letter to Gibson demanding answers "to a list of thirty questions," and made a drawing of Harrington's apartment, in order to demonstrate how forged letters might have been written on his friend's typewriter.[20]

It was also rumored that Gibson was actually in the service of the FBI or the CIA with the mission of creating discord among the expatriates.

It was this atmosphere of paranoia and suspicion in which Harrington and the others had to live that would lead him to entertain ideas that would once more place him in the spotlight of publicity in the U. S. Harrington has recounted the events that led up to it:

> One wintry weekend in 1960 I visited friends in Normandy. On Monday morning I returned to Paris where the concierge handed me a telegram which had arrived the night before. It was from Dick and simply said, "OLLIE PLEASE COME TO SEE ME AS SOON AS YOU GET THIS." It gave the name and location of a clinic I'd never heard of. Mystified, I phoned the clinic and asked to speak with Monsieur Richard Wright. I was told that it would not be possible. "Monsieur Wright died last night!"[21]

It had been Wright's habit to talk at length with either Harrington or Himes every morning by phone, a practice that sometimes strained their relationship, yet in this instance, neither had been informed of his intention to enter such a clinic. After the initial shock and the funeral, Harrington investigated all the circumstances of his friend's death at the same time that *Ebony* magazine cabled a request for an article on the subject. According to Himes, he helped Harrington outline and prepare the article, which appeared in the February 1961 issue as "The Last Days of Richard Wright."[22]

Harrington's rehearsal of the unanswered questions about the circumstances surrounding Wright's untimely death fueled speculation that it was an arranged assassination. The essay was also an admiring portrait of a dear friend, but it would serve as a touchstone for speculations that have never been resolved among Wright biographers. The issue became prominent again in 1977 when the unpublished part of Wright's autobiography *Black Boy*, dealing with his affiliation with the Communist Party, was published as *American Hunger*. In an article for the American Communist paper *Daily World*, Harrington more specifically identified political forces that might have made Wright's death desirable, especially his belief that Wright had never truly rejected Communism.[23]

Without Wright, things were not the same in Paris, and they had gradually been changing anyway. As Harrington later told a writer for *Esquire*, who was tracking down the last of what Norman Mailer had called the "hipsters":

> Once upon a time there was a small cafe called the Tournon . . . that became the headquarters of a group of people who gathered there—Dick Wright was one of them and Chester Himes was another. . . .Well, this group of people would sit around and swap tales at the Cafe Tournon, which would become a kind of place of refuge for them. There was a wonderful woman who ran the place called Madame Alazard, and it became a real family pad. . . . But then the death knell began to sound; Art Buchwald wrote a column on the place, and before very long the tourists would come and just sit around and stare at the real live hipsters and eventually the place, I understand, turned into something quite different.[24]

In pursuit of remunerative work, as usual, Harrington traveled to East Berlin in 1961 to accept an offer from the Aufbau Publishers to illustrate a series of American literary classics being translated into German. He settled into a small hotel room to work on the drawings when, one day in August, he suddenly found that history had caught up with him in a new way. Harrington has related the events:

> I heard a very sinister sound in the streets. I looked out of my tiny hotel window and down below there was a stream of tanks going along. They were Soviet tanks. That gave me a bad feeling because I'd seen that before.
>
> I went down out of my room and walked in the direction the tanks were going for about a mile. On the edge of a place which has since become known as Checkpoint Charlie there was a line of US tanks. I knew I was right in the middle of World War III. I had had enough of wars and I didn't want to be in the middle of any war after that. So, I went back to my hotel, but found that I couldn't leave because I didn't have the proper visas. The bureaucracy, the Cold War bureaucracy had really set in at that point. I was a virtual prisoner. I couldn't leave there. I lost my French apartment, I lost everything. I had to stay there.[25]

But Harrington had work and the prospect of more to come, so he settled in, not realizing that he was making a commitment for the duration of the Cold War.

The Germans in particular valued his skills as a political cartoonist, so he came to specialize in addressing the political situation in America and the world at large, with frequent attention to racism, poverty, and imperialism. Two publications used his work on a regular basis, the humor magazine *Eulenspiegel* and the general interest periodical *Das Magazine*, the last one of the most popular in East Germany. He was given the opportunity to work in color, which he had seldom had the chance to do, and at last his training as a painter coincided with his experience as a cartoonist to produce works both pointed in their satire and attractive in their balance of color and design.

His personal life took a positive turn when he visited a radio station to talk about writing some articles on the U. S. presidential race of 1964. In the office there, he met Helma Richter, who held a Ph.D. in economics but had left the academic world for more exciting work as a broadcast journalist. They would live together and eventually marry and have a son, Oliver, Jr.

When John Pittman, a black friend of Harrington's, became editor of the New York *Daily World* (formerly *The Worker*), he invited Harrington to contribute. His first editorial cartoons for the weekly paper appeared in the issue for 19 October 1968, one on the front cover and another in the magazine section, both reflecting on George Wallace and some racist statements recently made by the former Governor of Alabama and then presidential candidate. One or more cartoons by Harrington would remain a mainstay of the paper which reached 72,000 readers, many of whom came to look mainly for the cartoons and had less interest in the political content. In 1972, the *Daily World* published a portfolio of Harrington's cartoons called *Soul Shots*, with an introduction by fellow cartoonist Elton Fax, in recognition of his sixtieth birthday. He returned to the United States for the occasion, the first time in twenty years and until recently his only visit home.

It was in the *Daily World* cartoons and the color pages for the German magazines that Harrington's art reached its maturity. The Bootsie cartoons, while critical of society and human nature, were always indirect and depended on the corrective function of laughter, but the work of the last two decades has been brutally direct in its moral outrage. These have been the years of Vietnam, Watergate, the Nixon and Reagan administrations, the invasion of Grenada, the selling of arms to both Iran and Iraq, and public attention to the practice of apartheid in South Africa—events which have occupied the pens of political cartoonists here and the world over. While Harrington's have been specific and provocative in their acerbic criticism of policies and practices, they have been no more so than the cartoons found in many American publications. They have a strong affinity, in fact, with the cartoons published in the underground or alternative press publications of the 1960s.

One theme which has consistently occupied Harrington is institutionalized racism.

As an African-American, he has found it impossible as an artist not to be political: "Although I believe that 'art for art's sake' has its merits," he has written, "I personally feel that my art must be involved, and the most profound involvement must be with the Black liberation struggle."[26] His use of bold exaggeration and caricature, combined with a gritty evocation of reality, are powerfully attractive to the eye at the same time as they play on the political sensibility. His skillful use of color is almost seductive until the rude conjunction of style and content awakens the reader to the political and social contradictions being satirized. This is art with the edge of a razor.

Despite his forty years as an expatriate, Ollie Harrington has never considered himself anything other than an American. His avoidance of the Communist Party in Germany was a source of irritation to the authorities, but they tolerated him because of the enormous popularity of his cartoons. In fact, he became something of a cult figure when his work circulated among the students, professors, and intellectuals in East Germany. Many white German cartoonists were not pleased with having such a popular black American competitor. But the period of exile from the U. S. has been no great cause of concern for Harrington. He has written, "I'm fairly well convinced that one is an exile only when one is not allowed to live in reasonable peace and dignity as a human being among other human beings. Where one can give love and respect and receive the same from one's neighbors, one is no exile."[27] And he has always received both from those who have known him well whether in America, France, or Germany. Despite his physical absence for half of his life, Harrington is an important and influential figure in twentieth-century American culture, and his art will remain as a testament to the dignity of the human spirit in the face of racial oppression.

The intent of the present anthology is to document a part of Harrington's achievement, drawing on the resources of the Walter O. Evans collection of African-American art. All of the drawings included are reproduced directly from the originals. Most of the Bootsie cartoons derive from the late 1950s and 1960s, the *Daily World* editorial cartoons were drawn during the 1960s and 1970s, and the color cartoons were published in East German magazines during the 1970s and 1980s. Thus the volume provides an overview of his work during his years abroad, a time of intense productivity and mature accomplishment.

M. Thomas Inge

Notes

1. John D. Stevens, "'Bungleton Green': Black Comic Strip," *Journalism Quarterly*, 51 (Spring 1974), pp. 122–24. Also see Steven Loring Jones, "From 'Under Cork' to Overcoming Black Images in the Comics," in *Ethnic Images in the Comics* (Philadelphia: Balch Institute for Ethnic Studies, 1986), pp. 21–30, the only substantial essay on the subject of African-American cartoonists.

2. Interview with Oliver W. Harrington conducted by the author on 28 October 1992, at Colum-

bus, Ohio. This and the following address are the source of much of the biographical data in this introduction.

3. Address by Oliver W. Harrington at the 1992 Festival of Cartoon Art, Ohio State University, Columbus, Ohio, on 30 October 1992. The teacher called Miss McCoy here is called Miss Murray in Harrington's reminiscence, "Our Beloved Pauli," *Freedomways*, 11 (1971), p. 58.

4. Address.

5. Address.

6. These cartoons are preserved in clippings found in a set of anonymous scrapbooks in the Schomburg Center for Research in Black Culture of the New York City Library and were found by Christine McKay and Bonnie Gabowitz. Of the two cartoons from the *New York State Contender*, one is dated 22 October 1932, and the date has been torn from the second, but both relate to the same presidential race between Hoover and Roosevelt.

7. Ollie Harrington, "How Bootsie Was Born," *Freedomways*, 3 (1963), p. 519.

8. "How Bootsie Was Born," p. 520.

9. "Our Beloved Pauli," p. 62.

10. Langston Hughes, "Introduction," *Bootsie and Others* by Ollie Harrington (New York: Dodd, Mead, 1958), unpaged.

11. "Tradition and Technique Are Watchwords at Yale's School of Fine Arts," *Life*, 8 (12 February 1940), p. 44.

12. "Tradition and Technique," pp. 45–47.

13. Charles V. Hamilton, *Adam Clayton Powell, Jr.: The Political Biography of an American Dilemma* (New York: Atheneum, 1991), pp. 119–120, 105–106.

14. Keneth Kinnamon, *The Emergence of Richard Wright* (Urbana: University of Illinois Press, 1972), p. 148, note 85.

15. Hamilton, p. 185.

16. Oliver W. Harrington, *Where Is the Justice?* (Detroit: Walter O. Evans, 1991), p. 6. This is the first published text of the 1946 address. See also the quotations in "Clark Orders Lynching Case Be Presented to U.S. Jury," New York *Times*, 29 October 1946, pp. 1, 22.

17. "Bids Negro Fight for Place in Art," New York *Times*, 29 November 1946, p. 32.

18. Oliver W. Harrington, *Why I Left America* (Detroit: Walter O. Evans, 1991), p. 8.

19. John A. Williams, "My Man Himes: An Interview with Chester Himes," *Amistad 1* (New York: Vintage Books, 1970), p. 86. Also see Chester Himes, *My Life of Absurdity* (Garden City, NY: Doubleday, 1976), pp. 35–37.

20. Addison Gayle, *Richard Wright: Ordeal of a Native Son* (Garden City, NY: Anchor Press, 1980), pp. 282–283. Also see Michel Fabre, *The Unfinished Quest of Richard Wright* (New York: William Morrow, 1973), pp. 461–463, and Himes, *My Life of Absurdity*, p. 73.

21. Ollie Harrington, "The Mysterious Death of Richard Wright," *Daily World*, 17 December 1977, Magazine, pp. M4–M5.

22. Ollie Harrington, "The Last Days of Richard Wright," *Ebony*, 16 (February 1961), pp. 83–86, 88, 90, 92–94.

23. "The Mysterious Death of Richard Wright." Also see Terry Cannon, "Was Richard Wright Assassinated?" *Daily World*, 10 December 1977, p. 8.

24. Marion Magid, "The Death of Hip," *Esquire*, 63 (June 1965), pp. 101–102.

25. *Why I Left America*, pp. 12–13.

26. Ollie Harrington, "Look Homeward Baby," *Freedomways*, 13 (1973), p. 208.

27. "Look Homeward Baby," p. 207.

Bibliography

Works by Oliver W. Harrington

BOOKS AND PAMPHLETS

Bootsie and Others: A Selection of Cartoons by Ollie Harrington. New York: Dodd, Mead, 1958. Anthology of 88 cartoons.

Soul Shots: Political Cartoons by Ollie Harrington. New York: Long View Publishing, 1972. Portfolio of 16 cartoons originally published in the New York *Daily World*.

Where Is the Justice? Detroit: Walter O. Evans, 1991. Pamphlet with the text of a 1946 address to the New York Herald Tribune Forum.

Why I Left America. Detroit: Walter O. Evans, 1991. Pamphlet with the text of a 1991 address at Wayne State University.

Why I Left America and Other Essays. Edited by M. Thomas Inge. Jackson: University Press of Mississippi, 1993.

ARTICLES AND ESSAYS

"How Bootsie Was Born." *Freedomways*, 3 (1963), pp. 518–524. Reprinted in *Harlem USA*. John Henry Clarke, ed. New York: Collier, 1971. Pp. 72–79.

"The Last Days of Richard Wright." *Ebony*, 16 (February 1961), pp. 83–86, 88, 90, 92–94.

"Like Most of Us Kids." *Freedomways*, 16 (1976), pp. 255–257.

"Look Homeward Baby." *Freedomways*, 13 (1973), pp. 135–143, 200–215. Second part reprinted in *A Freedomways Reader*. Ernest Kaiser, ed. New York: International Publishers, 1976. Pp. 94–112.

"The Mysterious Death of Richard Wright." *Daily World*, 17 December 1977, Magazine, pp. M4–M5.

"Our Beloved Pauli." *Freedomways*, 11 (1971), pp. 58–63. Reprinted in *The Freedomways Reader*. Ernest Kaiser, ed. New York: International Publishers, 1976. Pp. 271–277.

"Southern Maneuvers." *The People's Voice*, 15 May 1943, p. 8; 22 May 1943, p. 8; 29 May 1943, p. 8

"Two Writers Look at *Through Black Eyes*." *Freedomways*, 14 (1974), pp. 154–157.

WORKS ILLUSTRATED

"Army Air Force." Pittsburgh *Courier*, 30 October 1943, p. 13. Full page with 8 illustrations and notes by Harrington.

Caine, Alfred E., ed. *Negro Heritage Reader for Young People*. Yonkers: Educational Heritage, 1965. Reprints *The Runaway Elephant* by Ellen Tarry, pp. 14–35, with 22 of the illustrations.

Clarke, John Henrik, ed. *Harlem USA*. New York: Collier, 1971. Reprints 4 cartoons.

Hughes, Langston. "Speak Well of the Dead." *Ebony*, 13 (October 1958), pp. 30–34. Essay with 6 illustrations.

Kaiser, Ernest, ed. *A Freedomways Reader*. New York: International Publishers, 1977. Cover painting in color.

Opportunity, 20 (December 1942), p. 365. Frontispiece: "An Enduring Peace and Democracy for All Men."

Sterling, Philip, ed. *Laughing on the Outside: The Intelligent White Reader's Guide to Negro Tales and Humor*. New York: Grosset & Dunlap, 1965. Reprints 5 cartoons from *Bootsie and Others*.
Tarry, Ellen. *Hezekiah Horton*. New York: Viking Press, 1942. Children's book with 34 illustrations.
Tarry, Ellen. *The Runaway Elephant*. New York: Viking Press, 1950. Children's book with 28 illustrations.
"Tradition and Technique Are Watchwords at Yale's School of Fine Arts." *Life*, 8 (12 February 1940), pp. 44–47. Reproduces in color the painting "Deep South," p. 46.

About Oliver W. Harrington

"America's Socio-Artist." *Opportunity*, 20 (December 1942), p. 365.
Aptheker, Herbert. "In Appreciation of Ollie Harrington." *Daily World*, 29 April 1980, pp. 8–9.
"Army Air Force." Pittsburgh *Courier*, 30 October 1943, p. 13.
"Bids Negro Fight for Place in Art." New York *Times*, 25 November 1946, p. 32.
Cannon, Terry. "Was Richard Wright Assassinated?" *Daily World*, 10 December 1977, p. 8.
Caswell, Lucy Shelton. "Oliver Harrington: A Biographical Sketch." *Cartoons and Ethnicity*. Columbus: Ohio State University Libraries,1992. Pp. 65–77. Also published as separate pamphlet, *Political Satire by Oliver Harrington*.
"Clark Orders Lynching Case Be Presented to U.S. Jury." New York *Times*, 29 October 1946, pp. 1, 22.
Dillard, Pam. "African American Expatriates Honored at Paris Conference." *The Southern Register*, Spring 1992, pp. 8–11.
Fabre, Michel. *From Harlem to Paris: Black American Writers in France, 1840–1980*. Urbana: University of Illinois Press, 1991.
Fabre, Michel. *The Unfinished Quest of Richard Wright*. New York: William Morrow, 1973. Second edition. Urbana: University of Illinois Press, 1993.
Gayle, Addison. *Richard Wright: Ordeal of a Native Son*. Garden City, NY: Anchor Press, 1980.
Hejc, Karel. "Ollie, Draw It!" *The Democratic Journalist*, 33 (March 1986), pp. 14–18.
Himes, Chester. *My Life of Absurdity*. Garden City, NY: Doubleday, 1976.
Hughes, Langston. "Introduction." *Bootsie and Others: A Selection of Cartoons by Ollie Harrington*. New York: Dodd, Mead, 1958. Unpaged.
Ivy, James W. "Mordant Satire." *The Crisis*, 65 (October 1958), pp. 523–524.
Johnson, Terry. "Ollie Harrington: Artist With Vision to Transform the World." *People's Weekly World*, 31 October 1992, pp. 11–13.
Jones, Steven Loring. "From 'Under Cork' to Overcoming: Black Images in the Comics." *Ethnic Images in the Comics*. Charles Hardy and Gail Stern, eds. Philadelphia: Balch Institute for Ethnic Studies, 1986. Pp. 21–30. Reprinted in *Nemo*, No. 28 (December 1987), pp. 16–21. Reprinted in *Black Ink*. San Francisco: Cartoon Art Museum, 1992. Pp. 5–15.
Kinnamon, Keneth. *The Emergence of Richard Wright*. Urbana: University of Illinois Press, 1972.
Magid, Marion. "The Death of Hip." *Esquire*, 63 (June 1965), pp. 89–103, 138.
Murphy, George B., Jr. "In the Freedom Family." *Freedom*, June 1951, p. 5.
Ransom, Llewellyn. "PV's Art Editor Ollie Harrington, Creator of 'Bootsie' and 'Pee Wee,' Enjoyed Life, Despite Setbacks." *The People's Voice*, 8 August 1942, p. 4.
Sloan, Lester. "The World According to Ollie." *Emerge*, 4 (November 1992), pp. 71–72.
Smythe, Hugh H. "*Bootsie and Others*." *Journal of Human Relations*, Summer, 1959, pp. 592–594.

Spencer, Andy. "Political Satire by Oliver Harrington." *Dialogue*, November/December, 1992, pp. 16–17.

Walker, Joe. "Ollie Harrington, Cartoonist, Celebrated for His Seriousness." *Muhammad Speaks*, 26 January 1973, pp. 13, 26; 2 February 1973, pp. 28–29.

Walker, Margaret. *Richard Wright: Daemonic Genius*. New York: Warner Books, 1968.

Williams, Ethel L. "A Tribute to the Negro War Correspondent." *Negro History Bulletin*, 8 (February 1945), pp. 110–118.

Williams, John A. "My Man Himes: An Interview with Chester Himes." *Amistad 1*. John A. Williams and Charles F. Harris, eds. New York: Vintage Books, 1970. Pp. 25–91.

Wolseley, Roland E. *The Black Press, U.S.A.* Ames: Iowa State University Press, 1971. Second edition, 1990.

"Say boy, I just wanted to say that I dont mind sittin' next to the coloreds at any old lunch-bar. Want'a try me out buddy?"

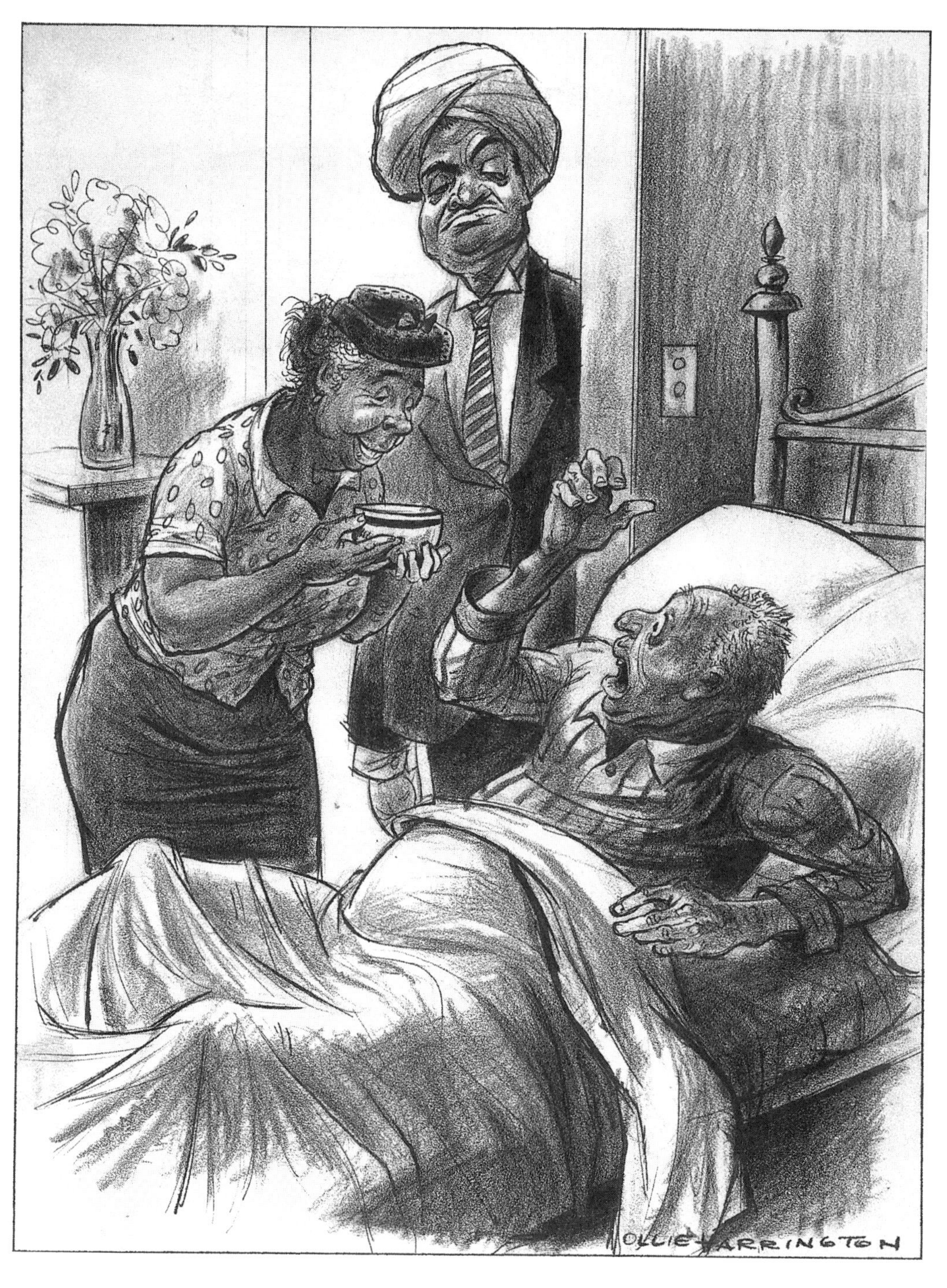

"This is a special medicine the professor brought all the way from Africa!"

"Ever since they put that red cross on his chest he's actin' jest like white folks when they see a cullud man enjoyin' his self . . . got to louse up the show!"

"Awright Bootsie, ev'rybody else laughs at my jokes 'cept you. What's wrong, you dont like cullud folks or som'p'n?"

"Rev, I'm real sorry I got to relieve you of that collection bag. But pray fer me boy, I'm just a stray sheep with some real weird complexes!"

"No, it dont make no sense to me neither Bootsie. But white folks jus' wont buy nothin' if it makes sense!"

"Yes honey, even Brother Bootsie was once a little baby with a mama who thought he was the cutest thing. But I guess you're too little to understand how *that* could be!"

"Sit right down Baby, I got somethin' to say to you. But I want'a be lookin' straight into your big brown eyes when I say it."

"I never thought I would live long enough to see my own daughter exposin' herself in front of a strange gentleman!"

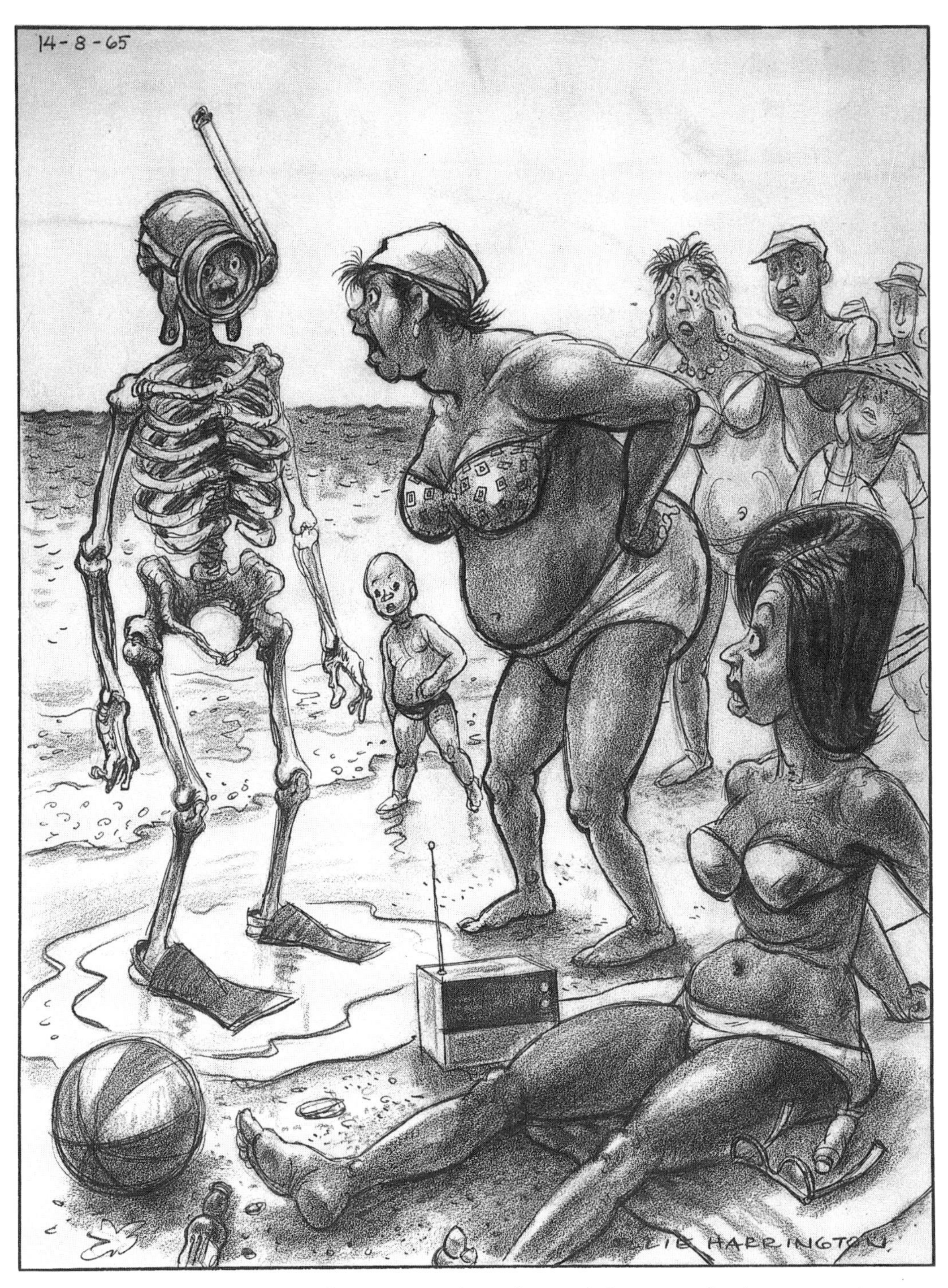

"Henry, I told you a million times that if you didn't stop foolin' around out there on the bottom of that ocean somethin' terrible was goin' to happen. Now just look at you!"

"Okay, we soon gon' let you freedom rahders out'a this lil' old jailhouse 'cause we gon' send ya'll to faght for freedom . . . *in Berlin*!"

"Now who would'a thought you martians was cousins? But you better not hang around here in Mississippi or the fools'll think you want to go to school"

"Man, do you realize that if we was in Alabama it would be aginst the law fer us cullud kids to walk on this stuff?"

"Well first of all you couldn't be Columbus 'cause the white folks wouldn't never let a cullud man discover America!"

"Boy, we used to get clobbered regular before integration. Now we're terrifyin' the whole goldurned league!"

"Looks like by the time these judges let us cullud kids get through school all the white kids will be fixin' to retire on old age pensions!"

"An' the next time the gov'mint asks us if we have registered any niggras to vote we can look 'em right in the eye an' answer 'Yes'!"

"Here Brother Bootsie, take this extra hammer I got here in case the gentlemens of the law decides that this demonstration is *too* peaceful!"

"Officer, what Alabama bar was you holed up in back in '44 when I was in Normandy protectin' your civil rights?"

"Whoooee Brother Bootsie, dig them Dade boys. They seem upset by sump'n that's takin' place in their shop. You realize what that *could signify*?"

"It's a cryin' shame Sis Dawkins. Them rascals down at the city hall wouldn't allow no carryin's on like this no place else except where us cullud folks lives!"

"Look man, I dont need you to tell me that they're only mermaids. An' I also happen to know that they got blonde hair, blue eyes, an' we're only three miles off the coast of South Carolina!"

"I dont care what the hell the NAACP thinks about it but I'm gettin' fed up. You've been doing this to me ever since that Patterson got knocked out!"

". . . an' why dont the NAACP make 'em stop usin' cullud boys to fight one 'nother. Dont they realize that causes a whole lot of confusion 'mongst us fight fans?"

"Hey, you knuckle-headed Uncle Tom, you. Aint you ashamed after strikin' out all of your own kinfolk?"

"White folks beatin' an' burnin' folks in Angola, chainin' 'em up in South Africa, so we gotta march buddy-o . . . to Berlin!"

"Congratulations Sergeant Smith. You're to be the first man shot to the moon. It's sort of a goodwill gesture to our African friends!"

"One drop of this stuff behind your ear . . . and just watch the menfolk run amuck!"

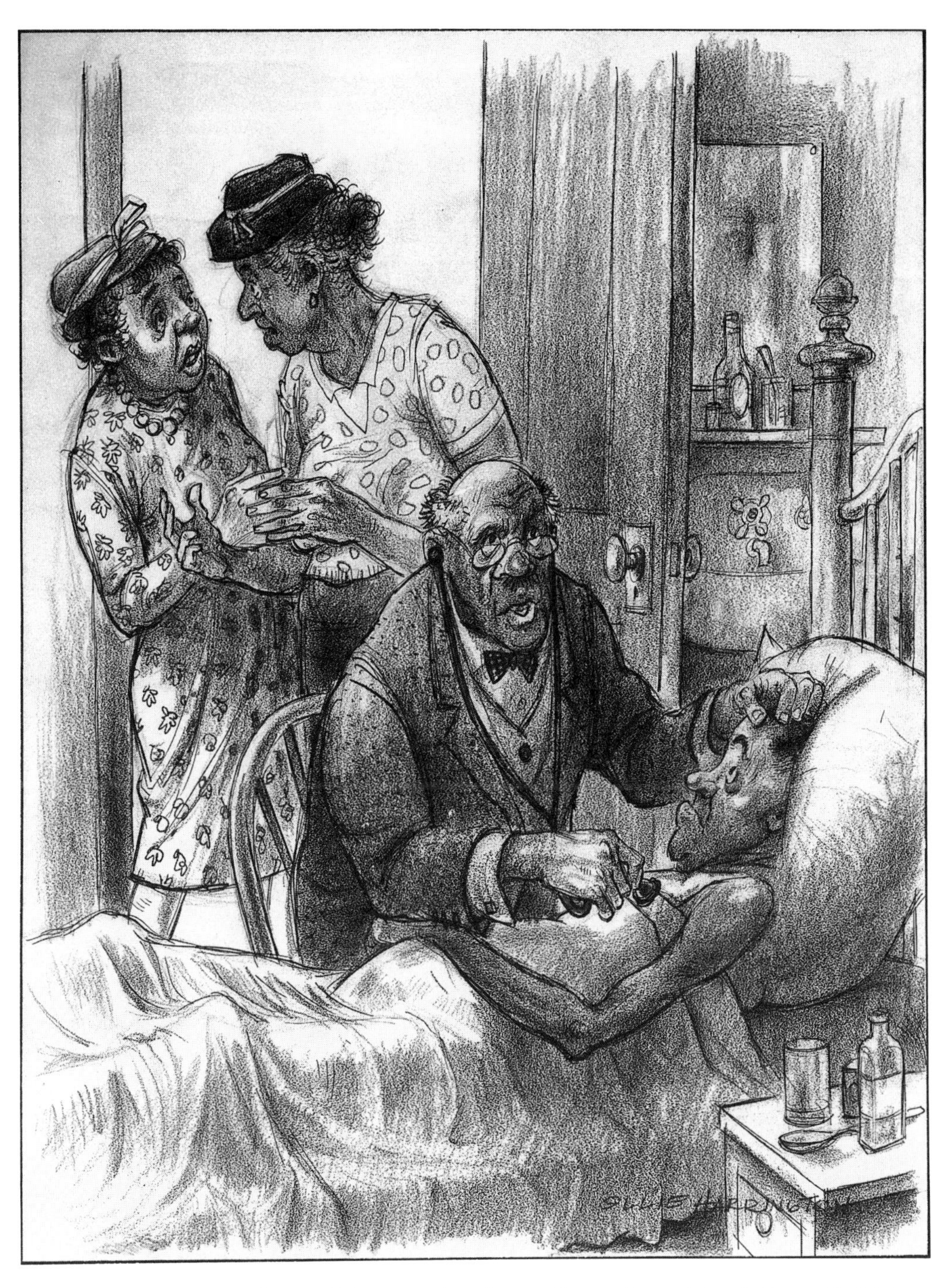

"His health was perfect 'till he got that letter from the white folks tellin' him he was goin' to be the first cullud man on a jury that's goin' to try them Klu Kluxers!"

"White chil'rens mamas buys 'em all the candy they can eat. But you cullud mamas just aint ready for integration, I guess!"

"Henry, I just knew somethin' was wrong the minute the white folks let us in here without makin' a big fuss!"

"Why caint folks realize that we're only tryin' to keep the free world pure?"

OLLIE HARRINGTON

PEOPLE'S DAILY WORLD

"Well natcherly I know whut I wanna be when I grow up but statistics say I aint gon' git to grow up!"

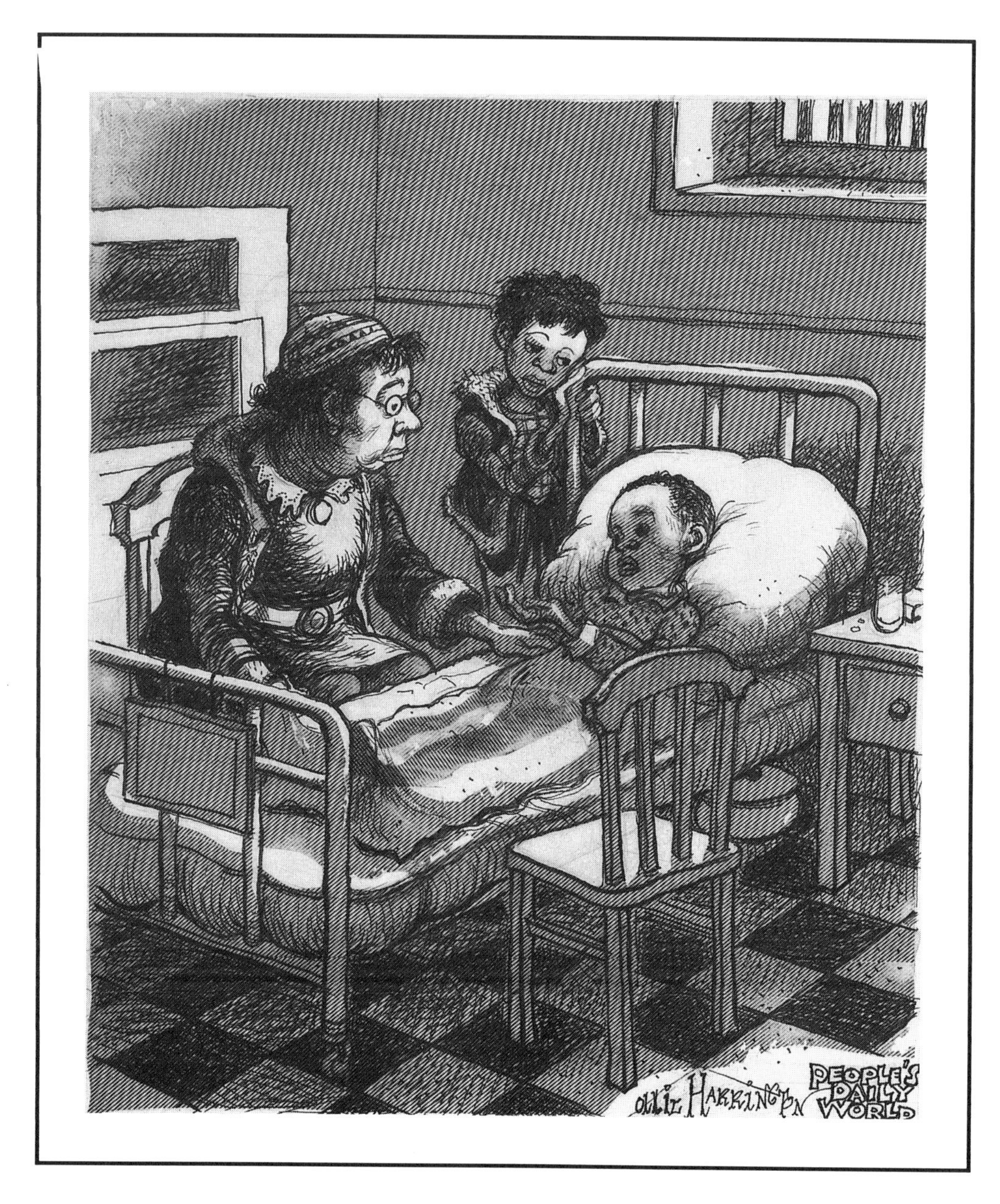

"Coach advised joggin' but the cops say I was fleein' the scene of a crime!"

"SPCA took my puppy away last night. Said it was cruel to subject helpless animals to conditions like this!"

"Bet'cha one thing. If there is a Santa Claus an' he ever shows up here he better be wearin' a baseball catcher's mask!"

"Hey man, you reckon that dude in there realize how lucky he is?"

"Hey you! How come ya never show stuff that gives us ethnics a square shake?"

"My family was missin' for three whole days 'till I remembered Ma said we was movin' our blankets an' things three subway stations further south!"

"How come all the good people on the tv always live in them great mansions while the creeps all live like us?"

"Ya can find a lot'a eatable scraps out here if you can remember what they was supposed to teach you about germs in the biology class!"

"What'a we gon' say when them badmouth third world lawyers start askin' how come this is still crimeville when practically all the young blacks is in the slammer?"

Blind leading the blind!

"Sorry ol' buddy, but we're cuttin' the deficit . . . meanin' you!"

1987—year of the homeless!

State of the Union!

'Commonwealth' games: gold, silver and bronze!

"Ron, she's fillin' faster'n we can bail 'er . . . so . . . who do we throw overboard next?"

Gunsmoke!

"Okay, okay, but they were the first who dug my great crusade against communism thing!"

FULL PARDON
RONALD REAGAN
HELMUT KOHL
OLLIE HARRINGTON
DAILY WORLD

No point in even slowin' down here, Ron. These people been readin' *The Daily World* or sump'n!

"Better radio his helicopter not to land account of aint nobody showed up except the town's two leadin' drunks!"

STAR WARS PROGRAM
CORPORATIONS TENDING BIDS FOR SOME OF THE ACTION IN THIS TRILLION DOLLAR RIP-OFF ARE URGED TO KEEP COST OVER-RUNS AT A SANE LEVEL.
★★★★★★★★★★★
WHITE HOUSE
DOW
$
Ollie Harrington
DAILY WORLD

". . . And Ed Meese, over at justice, has documentary evidence linkin' anti-Contra senators with Dracula . . . uh . . . I mean with the Kremlin!"

"Momma, is that what Reagan has in mind when he says that unemployment is droppin'?"

"Baby! Are you tryin' to tell me that they're willin' to risk startin' World War III because a coup'la homeless, jobless, hopeless fellers like us forgot to say 'no'?"

FREE ENTERPRISE
$
$
Ollie Harrington
DAILY WORLD

SOCIAL SECURITY
OLLIE HARRINGTON
DAILY WORLD

To the Star Wars!

For some . . . crime doesn't always pay!

AIDS
CRACK
ANTI MINORITIES
UNION BUSTING
WALL ST
OLLIE HARRINGTON
PEOPLE'S DAILY WORLD

"That's lawyer Dandridge, Bush's latest choice to head the civil rights thing. But man, even the neighborhood dogs is outraged!"

"We conned the media with some kind'a secret military mission stuff but the only secret is that we're leavin' Dan Quayle out here where he cant possibly goof!"

ANTI-
SOVIET
TERROR
CIA
OLLIE HARRINGTON
DAILY WORLD

WHITE HOUSE SPOKESMEN CLAIM THAT MASSIVE AIR-SEA STRIKES AGAINST LIBYA WERE TRIGGERED BY THE DISCOVERY OF AN ALLEGED LIBYAN PLOT TO DESTROY THE ENTIRE U.S. SIXTH FLEET!
39
OLLIE HARRINGTON
DAILY WORLD

IRAQUI AIR FORCE
DONATED BY CIA
IRANIAN AIR FORCE
GIFT OF CIA
OLLIE HARRINGTON
PEOPLE'S DAILY WORLD

EXIT TO
WEST BERLIN
AIDS
CRACK
Ollie Harrington
PEOPLE'S
DAILY
WORLD

1933-1945
WE THE LIVING MUST NEVER FORGET THE MANY MILLIONS OF ALL RACES AND RELIGIONS WHO VANISHED INTO THE 'MASTER RACE' INFERNO.
Ollie Harrington
PEOPLE'S DAILY WORLD

SAVE THE WILD BEASTS OF OUR FORESTS FROM CRUEL EXTINCTION!
... THE RHINOS AND ELEPHANTS
OLLIE HARRINGTON
PEOPLE'S DAILY WORLD

"The Nordamericanos tore up poor Moreno's contract because he bungled three assassination assignments!"

Final result—Fat Cats: 1,000,000,000, People: 0

THE DAILY WHOPPER
BUSH, THATCHER SEE END OF COMMUNISM
SPECULATORS LAND DELOPERS JUBILANT: STOCKS SOAR
FRENCH, GERMAN NEO-NAZIS JOINED
RACISM
ECOLOGY
AIDS
CRACK
OLLIE HARRINGTON
PEOPLE'S DAILY WORLD

CONSTRUCTIVE ENGAGEMENT
APARTHEID
Ollie HARRINGTON
PEOPLE'S DAILY WORLD

Lift-off!

News item: South Africa has announced that only blacks who are not on 'suspect' lists may attend funerals of police victims!

REFORM PROGRAM FOR IMPROVING THE QUALITY OF EDUCATION FOR BLACKS.
SOUTH AFRICAN GOV'T. MINISTRY OF EDUCATION
PEOPLE'S DAILY WORLD

News item: South African authorities announce exciting, new plans for encouraging 'racial harmony'!

'Constructive engagement'!

APARTHEID
ANC
OLLIE HARRINGTON
PEOPLE'S DAILY WORLD

"Sic the naughty man, dahling!"

"General, this morning's underground test was super. But, sir, we cant seem to find any trace of Texas, Arizona, New Mexico or Nevada on our satellite photos!"

"Gentleman, what'cha gotta realize in this game is ya cant win 'em all!"

"Can anyone out there hear me? Hurrah! I think our side won!!"

"That one didn't go off but 60,000 others did . . . though 200 would have emptied the planet anyway!"

"That guy who says he can identify the cops who shot them unarmed teen-agers last week got busted by the feds in one'a their famous sting operations!"

"Dear Mom please don't worry. I have a nice, warm place for the winter right under the snootiest hotel in New York. . . ."

UNITED STATES OF
VIVA
OLLIE HARRINGTON

"I never seen the streets so empty. They must be givin' away free crack someplace!"

Practice makes perfect!

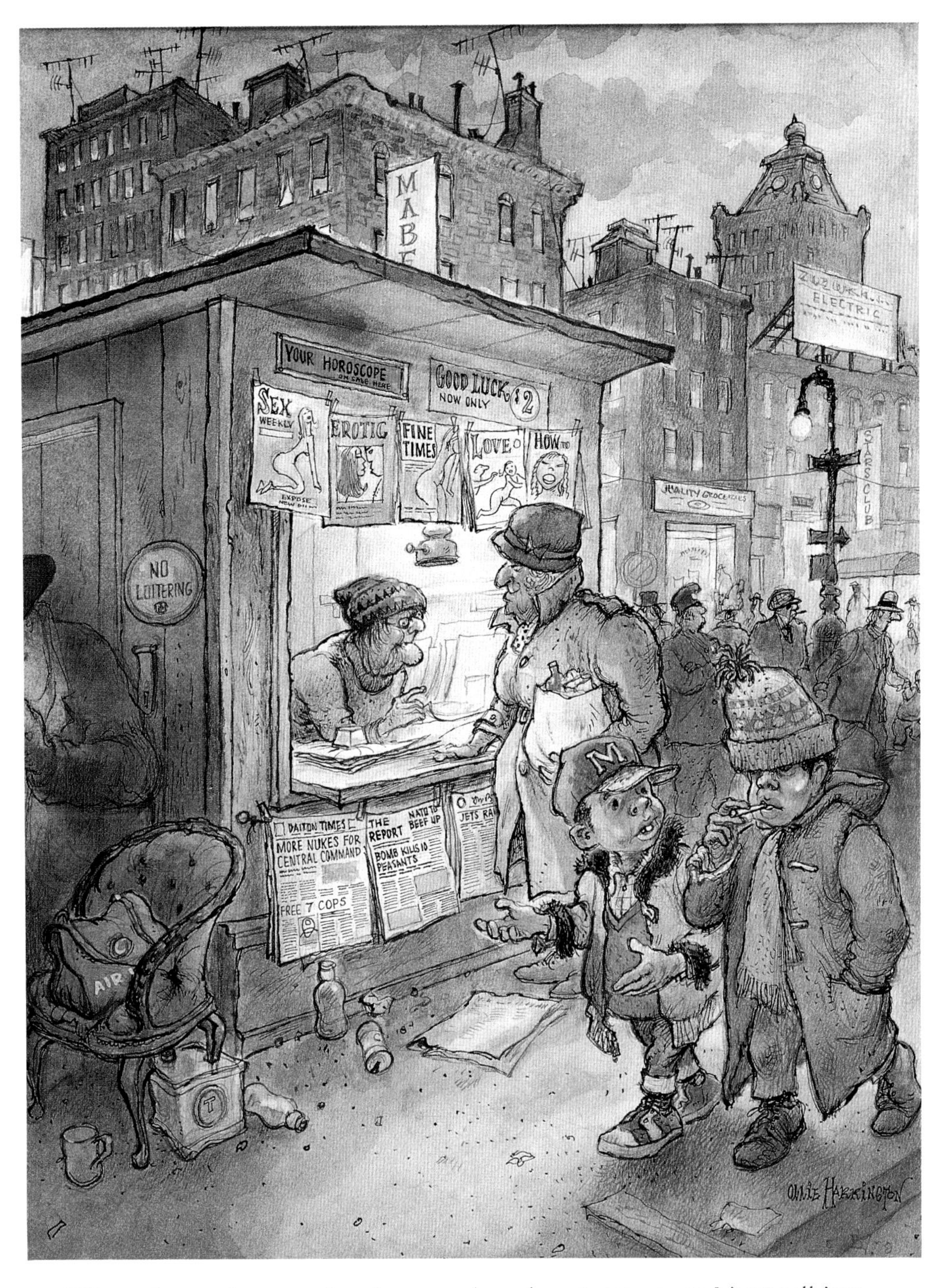

"When they asks me what I wanna be when I grows up I just tell 'em, alive man, tha's all!"

"The city set up this warm place for freezin' house pets, but they won't take in us freezin' pet owners!"

"Sarge, I just caught this gangster tryin' to break in here where he could steal this animal's meat!"

"Nobody of that name sleeps here permanent, but why dontcha try behind the supermarket?"

Bible belt

"Now don't go bothering your papa. He's had a hard day firing 2000 people in his factory."

War on drugs

"No madame, this aint the annual marathon. These people just heard rumours about a few job openin's downtown!"

"My educated uncle says we're upper class because we still have a roof over our heads!"

"And remember what the photo instructor at the Forest Hills Photo Group always said: 'In bright sunshine, always use a fast shutter'."

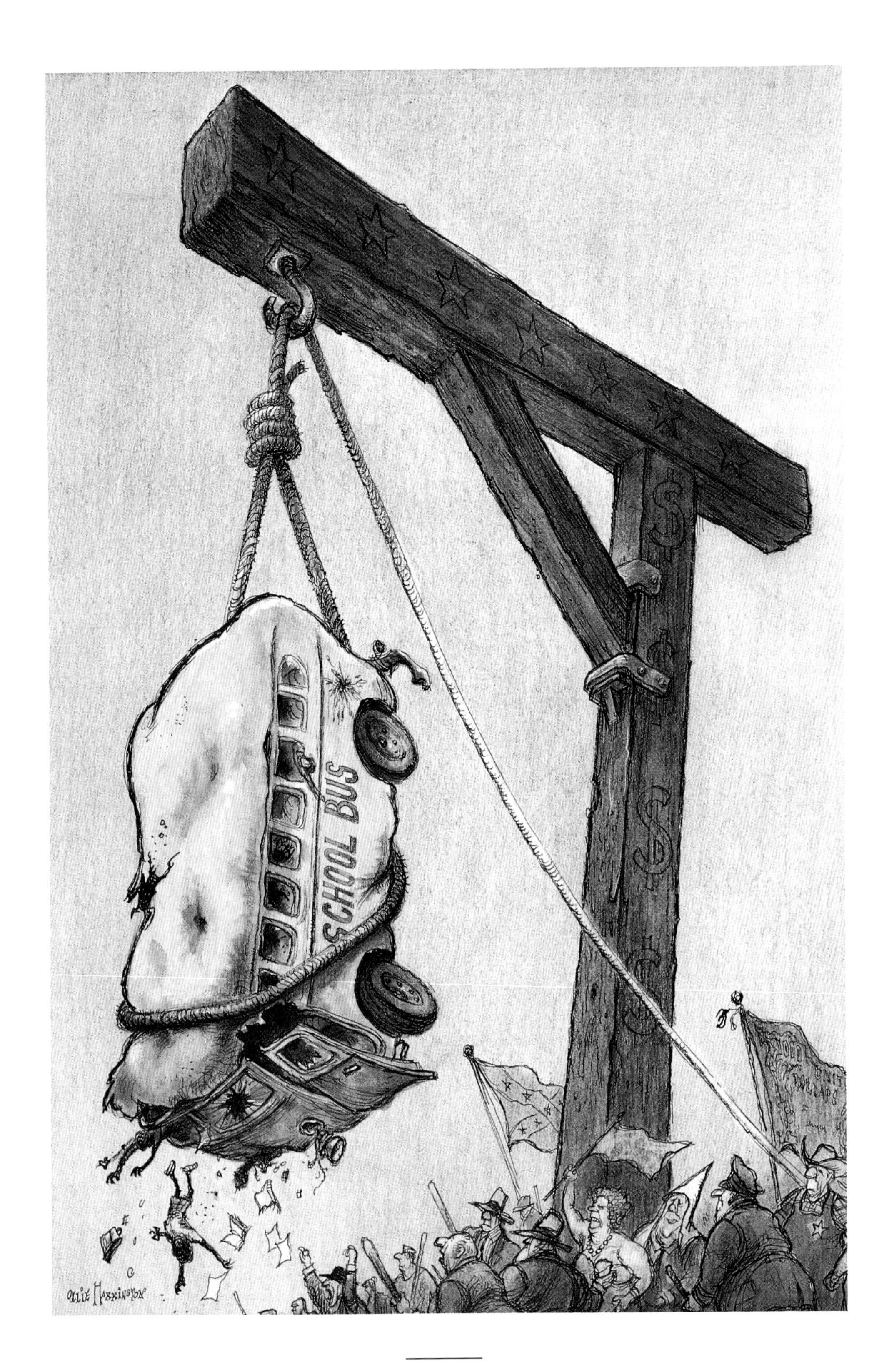
SCHOOL BUS
OLLIE HARRINGTON

"A fantastic talent, sir. He has kept the whole family eating regular since I got laid off two years ago!"

"He's fantastically talented, honey. In fact the government is trying to steal him from the Mafia!"

LIBERTYVILLE
68
ROCCO SONS
CONTRACTORS

"We give their pay to the Junta because they'd only waste it on whiskey and women!"

"Hey tone it down will you amigo. We got one of them Yanqui human rights groups upstairs interviewing the general!"

"That absent-minded mayor gave him a twenty percent cut in the numbers racket uptown without first consultin' the Mafia!"

"You boys done a great job bringin' democracy to the island Cap'n. Looks like back home already!"

"Hey Conchita, Washington now says we can only use our Contra pay on strictly non-military activities . . . !"

"Let's vote on this in a democratic way, girls. Do we give credit to the poor ex-Contras?"

"It is most unsporting but then the third world people must be made to see that there are two sides to everything."

UNITED STATES OF
VIVA
OLLIE HARRINGTON

News Item: Postal officials have hastened to assure the public that full mail deliveries would be maintained in the event of a nuclear war.